HERITAGE
AND PROMISE

HERITAGE
AND PROMISE

Emmert F. Bittinger

The Brethren Press
Elgin, Illinois

HERITAGE AND PROMISE

Copyright © 1970, 1983 by The Brethren Press,
Elgin, Illinois 60120

First Edition, 1970
Revised Edition, 1983

Cover painting by Guy Wolek

Library of Congress Cataloging in Publication Data

Bittinger, Emmert F., 1925-
    Heritage and Promise.

    Bibliography: p.
    Includes index.
    1. Church of the Brethren. I. Title.
BX7821.2.B54 1983   289.7'3   83-4624
ISBN O-87178-357-6

Printed in the United States of America

Contents

Preface

The study of history is valuable to our understanding of the present. And yet, knowledge of our denominational background has not been widely enough disseminated to Brethren people. Strangely, this is not because our church does not have many highly qualified and very active historians at work. Perhaps, we have never had more research and publication of church history than now. The past fifteen years have seen a phenomenal outpouring of books and articles dealing with our origin and background as a church.

Unfortunately, the layman seldom has access to much of this material. Yet, knowledge of our past and understanding of denominational development is basic to our commitment as Christians and to our obtaining of a sense of direction. Because of this need, a small and inexpensive publication presenting our denominational story is much needed. It is the hope of the author that many study groups, classes, and individuals who have never before held a Brethren history in their hands will now have ready and easy access to such a book. Our heritage is precious and worth knowing. This book, therefore, is dedicated to the reader.

The author does not claim to have contributed to original research in putting this book together. This was not required for its purpose of making existing knowledge available to the average reader. So much has been produced by our professional historians in recent years that it was a difficult enough task to select from the material available. If there is originality, it is mainly in what is selected, the way it is organized, and the evaluations and emphases. The idea of the diagram entitled "Circle of Christian Doctrine" is original, but Lori Lineweaver created the design. Experience with independent invention, however, has shown that all too often a claim to originality is unfounded because of ignorance of the work of others!

A book of this sort is dependent on a host of other historians and their writing. Careful attention was given to the duty and the pleasure of acknowledging sources. Hopefully, there are no major omissions or failures at this point. The author is grateful to several individuals for the loan of resources. To William G. Willoughby and to Robert F. Eshelman thanks are given for the use of valuable unpublished materials.

To Donald F. Durnbaugh appreciation is expressed for his reading of the manuscript and for his tactful and helpful suggestions. Dr. Durnbaugh, whose own research and publication has greatly enriched our knowledge of the past, also kindly permitted a disproportionate use to be made of his published materials. A sincere acknowledgment is given to Ora W. Garber, book editor, and to Ercell V. Lynn, curriculum adviser. Their expert assistance in preparing the first edition was at all times needed and generously given.

To my father, Foster M. Bittinger, now deceased, and to my teacher, Dr. Floyd E. Mallott, from both of whom I obtained an enduring love of Brethren history, grateful acknowledgment is given. Last, and first, credit and appreciation are due to Esther, my wife, who not only gave many hours of typing but gave generously of her moral support as well.

Emmert F. Bittinger

Bridgewater, Virginia
July 1982

1

From Rome
to Schwarzenau

Prologue

The appearance of the Brethren in Schwarzenau, Germany, in 1708, is not isolated from other historical events of the times. In fact, the decision of Alexander Mack and seven others to break with the existing churches can be understood best as a part of the general religious and moral unrest which had long existed in western Europe. Anyone attempting to comprehend the reasons why the baptism in the Eder River took place will need to wrestle with larger questions pertaining to events leading up to those years. For example, why did the Pietistic movement arise? Why did rebaptizers, the reformers, and other groups working for renewal of the church gain so much influence? Indeed, why did these movements become possible at all? What was happening religiously, socially, and educationally in the years prior to 1708? In what way are these happenings related to the dissatisfactions which led Martin Luther to proclaim his reforms in 1517, nearly two centuries before?

These questions are fascinating to all those persons interested in understanding reasons for the faith that is in them. It is thrilling to see events unfold and lead into succeeding ones. It is gratifying to discover the pattern which underlies and supports the birth of our denomination and its sister denominations—and to find out that the founders were responsible men and women who were struggling intellectually and emotionally with issues which were wracking the social order of their day. Perhaps significant lessons for our contemporary times will become apparent to us as we assess the thoughtful and difficult decisions of those who sought to take their faith seriously in the turbulent period during and just after the seventeenth century.

Comprehension of this story will go a long way toward correcting the historical and theological illiteracy which allegedly afflicts the membership of our churches. As we participate in the unfolding of the pages from our denominational past, we shall gain familiarity with and begin to assimilate the fundamental aspects of our heritage. We shall gain confidence and "be with it" when it comes to discussing and sharing with others our Brethren beliefs and practices. Perhaps some of the strangeness and the alienation which many youth and newly received members from other denominations feel in the presence of our ordinances will be lessened.

Even more important, as we become acquainted with the costly solutions proposed by the religious leaders of the seventeenth and eighteenth centuries to the social and religious disorders of their day, we may be led to grapple more seriously with those of our time. Lastly, it is hoped that this survey will result in renewed insights into the way in which God works to express his love and purpose in the common life of his people.

Conditions Leading to the Protestant Reformation

Prior to the sixteenth century only the Catholic Church was recognized in Europe. Two kinds of authority and power existed side by side: the religious power, residing in the church and in the person of the pope; and the secular power, residing in the state and in the persons of kings and emperors. Sometimes these powers were joined into a single force which effectively controlled the people. At other times these powers contested for control. Sometimes the church was ascendant over the kings, who were then subject to religious edict. At other times, the kings and the emperors united against the pope and defeated his armies. The pope came to believe that all political and secular authorities should be subject to the church. Religious power was sometimes abused or used arbitrarily with degrading results upon the church and the people.

The power of the Catholic Church reached its height during the years 1198-1216, the period when Innocent III was pope. During this time, kings and emperors did obeisance to the pope and all people acknowledged him as their superior and as the earthly representative of God. During the period in which the church enjoyed the peak of both secular and religious favor it conducted successful wars against opposing groups, sought to suppress heresy by torture and death, and received vast sums of money from all its subjects in Europe. Many degrading and unchristian social, political, and religious practices, most of them regarded as normal at the time, came into the life of the church.

Because of various abuses and miscalculations, the papacy began a long decline between the fourteenth and the seventeenth century. Many factors contributed to this decay. The papacy suffered military defeats. The king of France refused to permit large sums of money to be sent to Rome. In 1303 his forces seized the pope and imprisoned him. During this century, the papacy was transferred from Rome to France, where it became subservient to state interests.

Other events took place in succeeding years to weaken further the influence of the church. Reforming movements arose. The Albigenses and the Waldenses, who stressed the scriptural authority and basis for Christian life and doctrines, had already been successfully put down in the twelfth century. In the fourteenth century, William of Occam (1280-1349),[1] a respected theologian, revived some of the major claims of the Waldensians—that the pope is not infallible and that the Bible is the only and final authority in matters of faith and conduct. These and similar views were taken up by other voices calling for purification. John Wycliffe (1320-1384), known for his translation of some of the Scriptures into English, preached against the corruption within the church. Acknowledging the

---

[1]In Chapter 1, birth and death dates of persons referred to are given so as to assist the reader in orienting himself within the long time-period covered.

Bible as the final source of truth, he opposed the pope. In 1401, possession of an English Bible was made punishable by death and the followers of Wycliffe were forcibly suppressed.

In Prague, John Hus (1369-1415), a professor and powerful preacher, was burned at the stake for denouncing the excesses of the church. He too claimed the Bible as the highest authority. Even in Italy, the stronghold of the church, voices were being raised against the evils within the church. In Florence, Savonarola (1452-1498), a popular and influential preacher and acquaintance of Michelangelo, opposed the authority of the pope; he was condemned, tortured, and burned at the stake in 1498.

Before 1500, the church was too powerful to be greatly threatened by these scattered prophets who courageously opposed wrong as they saw it. But, other developments were gradually taking place to change this. One of these developments was the Renaissance, which began in Italy in the fourteenth century and gradually spread over all of Europe. The result of this was a great transformation of the life and the culture of the people.

Scientific inventions took place which enabled industry to prosper and thus increase the wealth and the population of the cities. Shipping and world exploration became feasible, opening up new vistas of the globe for the scholars to ponder. Education and learning, which once had been the exclusive domain of monastic communities and clergy, began to be sought after by the nonclergy as well. With growing education came greater stress upon the local language and literature. This in turn stimulated the growth of patriotism and nationalism, which led to further weakening of papal political authority. Art, sculpture, architecture, and painting began to free the human spirit into greater individualism and self-expression. Rationalism, grappling with historical and practical problems, produced a critical outlook and subjected many superstitions and religious claims to doubt and ridicule. The study of Greek and Hebrew was revived. This enabled both secular and religious scholars to advance their critical knowledge of the Bible and to lay the foundations for new translations. The invention of printing enabled more people to have access to devotional and scriptural material.

In short, between the twelfth and the fifteenth centuries, the life and the culture of Europe were undergoing great transition. As a result of these changes, those forces seeking to reform the church were strengthened. The political, intellectual, and spiritual monopoly of the church was weakened. Protest against the church was becoming more intense and vocal. Lacking the ability to predict the future, no one could possible have foreseen the startling events which soon were to transform the church and the religious scene in Europe in the sixteenth century. Neither could anyone have succeeded in preventing those changes.

The Protestant Reformation

The beginning of the Protestant Reformation is generally dated in 1517 when Martin Luther (1483-1546) nailed his ninety-five theses to the church door at Wittenberg. Although this may seem to us to be a radical act, Luther did not foresee that this act would be regarded as an attack on the pope and eventually would lead to his (Luther's) becoming a fugitive. He did not intend to found a new church.

A man of peasant origins, Luther had become an Augustinian monk in the Catholic Church. Even though his vows were extreme and his penance severe, he did not find peace for many years. Finally, an experience of renewal gave him new enthusiasm and power as a religious leader. The head of the monastery thereupon sent him to Wittenberg, where he preached at the university. Utterly sincere, he was dissatisfied with many practices of the Catholic Church, some of which had been criticized for centuries.

Luther became especially angry with the intensive pressure put upon the ignorant peasants to buy indulgences so that the pope would have enough funds to build St. Peter's cathedral in Rome. The doctrine of indulgences taught that the pope could grant forgiveness to the sinner, thus shortening the stay of the sinner in purgatory. The poor spent much-needed money for these assurances. In addition, Luther's ninety-five theses stressed justification by faith, the authority of the Bible, the priesthood of all believers, and the important role of the Holy Spirit. Luther also claimed that God directly forgives those who are sincere and he appealed to scriptural authority in support of his claims, thus downgrading the authority of the sacred traditions of the church.

The ninety-five theses were printed and widely read all over Germany, achieving a distribution not possible for materials of this sort in earlier times. Luther's ideas gained wide support and acceptance in Germany, and this fact probably explains why he did not suffer torture and death as did martyrs such as Hus and Savonarola. Luther was tried and found guilty by the church, but he was protected from the fury of the religious court. It seemed as though all of Germany had been waiting for someone to put into words what everyone was thinking but was afraid to say about the sale of indulgences and about other abuses. Eventually, however, the followers of Luther were cut off from the Catholic Church by the Council of Trent (1545-1563) and became the Lutheran Church.

Luther's fame spread to other European countires, Switzerland became a second powerful center of the Reform movement. A parish priest at Zurich, Ulrich Zwingli (1484-1531), who had become familiar with the writings of both Luther and the humanist scholar Erasmus (1467-1536), began to preach strongly against abuses within the church. In addition, he gave his flock new knowledge by instructing them directly from the Bible, which he regarded as the final authority for the church. He, like Luther, opposed the sale of indulgences and the worship of relics of the saints.

The reform that Zwingli promoted was much more far-reaching than that of Luther. Zwingli said that the Bible did not require priests to be celibate. He repudiated the Catholic doctrine that the bread and the wine became the body and the blood of Christ in the Mass, claiming that the Communion was merely a service of remembrance. Seeking to modify the practices of the church so that they included only those things expressly commanded in the New Testament, Zwingli removed from the churches all pictures, tapestries, candles, ornaments, and even organs. Although Mass was continued, the sermon, spoken in the language of the people, was made the heart of the service.

The reform movement was gaining rapid momentum. Some aspects of the movement went much faster than either Luther or Zwingli desired. For example, in Zurich, a group of Protestants began to claim that Christ had been baptized as an adult. They asserted that infant baptism was not supported in the New Testament and was nothing but a convenient invention of the church. All Christians should be baptized as adults so that they can openly declare their faith and experience conversion. Those who promoted these beliefs were called Anabaptists, meaning rebaptizers. Zwingli emphatically opposed them. Under his leadership they were persecuted and driven out of the city. However, their beliefs did not disappear. Later a converted priest from Holland, Menno Simons (1492-1559), joined the Anabaptist movement and gave it wise and practical leadership. Menno Simons became the founder of the Mennonites, who continued to be called Anabaptists.

France was not untouched by the spirit of renewal sweeping Europe. John Calvin (1509-1564), of Catholic background, and a student at the University of Paris, began secretly to read the forbidden writings of Luther. He became convinced that Luther was right. Upon joining a group of Protestants he was twice arrested and imprisoned. He lost the opportunity for a promising career as a lawyer. He decided to go to Switzerland where greater safety was granted to Protestants. At the age of twenty-six, he published the *Institutes of the Christian Religion,* which became one of the most powerful books of the Reformation.

Although Zwingli was dead when Calvin came to Geneva in 1536, they had many ideas in common. Because of Calvin's dedicated ministry and preaching, Geneva became a stronghold of Protestantism. Calvin stressed the moral life and must be recognized for ridding the city of many horrible and injurious customs. He demanded strict obedience. In his congregation one could be fined for laughing or sleeping in church and imprisoned for rolling dice or wearing fashionable clothes. Each congregation was ruled by elected elders who met in a meeting called the Presbytery. The Presbyterians trace their origin back to Calvin in Geneva. Also, Reformed churches in Europe and America regard Zwingli and Calvin as their founders.

By 1545, the Protestant movement had been well planted in Germany, Switzerland, France, Holland, and England. The Catholic Church had lost much which it now sought to gain back in a vigorous effort which is called the Counter-Reformation. This took place in the latter half of the sixteenth century, just as the Protestant Reformation was reaching its height. A council of the Catholic Church was called at Trent, a city near the northern border of Italy. This council met off and on until 1563. Its first achievement was to demand that all Protestants reunite with the Catholic Church and conform to its doctrines. Since the Protestants refused to concede, a "holy war" was launched against them in Germany and they were defeated by the Catholic forces. Although neither Catholics nor Protestants were willing to make significant concessions, many Catholic leaders acknowledged the need for genuine reforms within their church.

As a consequence of the Counter-Reformation, the Catholic Church gained in three areas: (1) organizing of efforts to combat and negate Protestant doctrine, (2) bringing about some needed reforms in the life of the church (there have been no corrupt popes since the Counter-Reformation), (3) alignment of political and religious personnel to fight against Protestant gains. It is worth noting that during this period a small but ineffectual minority of Catholic leaders was stressing (as were the Protestant critics) the need for elevating the authority of the Holy Scriptures, for a return to the religious teachings of the early church fathers, and for genuine church reform. Although these ideas were put down, it is interesting to speculate on the effect that these proposed reforms of Catholicism might have had on the direction of Catholic-Protestant relations. At any rate, the Counter-Reformation had the effect of slowing down the rapid gains of Protestantism as a mass movement. However, hostility and repression continued to mark the relations of the two religious bodies throughout the seventeenth century.

Between 1618 and 1648, Europe's bloodiest religious wars broke out. Protestants revolted against Catholic political and religious controls in Prague by murdering two Catholic regents. This revolt spread quickly, and soon Germany, Austria, and Hungary were enmeshed in horrible interreligious strife and open warfare. This continued until both sides had their populations greatly reduced, their people brutalized, the fields and towns destroyed, and the remnants of Christian virtue and sentiment all but eradicated. Christian life in Europe had fallen to a new low-water mark. Protestants and Catholics alike, in seeking by evil means to force their beliefs on the opposite side, succeeded only in bringing the life of western Europe to the brink of destruction.

The Treaty of Westphalia (1648) brought the open warfare to a conclusion by providing Lutherans, Reformed, and Catholics equal civil and religious rights in Germany and Switzerland. However, each state or province in Germany was to be *totally* Lutheran, Reformed, or Catholic according to the decree of the head of each state. The people were forced to accept an officially proclaimed religion under threat of persecution or to migrate to another province. A new foundation was laid for continued religious intolerance under the protective wing of local governments. Furthermore, state protection and religious monopoly did not encourage vital religious experience, evangelistic activity, enlivened preaching, or church services geared to the needs of the people. Religious mediocrity and loss of creativity settled upon Catholic and Protestant churches alike. The years 1650 to 1750 were a time of theological conservatism and orthodoxy within the established churches. The Reformation had become bogged down at the point of gaining an empty victory for certain doctrinal changes. The renewal of the spiritual life of the clergy and the laity was yet far distant. Religious intolerance and rejection of new insights were commonplace. Maintenance of the status quo and enforcement of religious and doctrinal conformity became important values.

The Crowded Road to Schwarzenau

As one looks back from the vantage point of history, it appears that the arrangements of the Treaty of Westphalia and the conditions of the latter half of the seventeenth century constituted a fertile and productive soil for carrying certain aspects of the Protestant Reformation much further. Two movements in particular prospered in those years of injustice, persecution, and near anarchy. The first was the much older Anabaptist movement which survived from the previous century and which took a new lease on life in the years just prior to 1700. The other movement, that of the Pietists, was a unique combining of certain older Protestant ideas of spiritual renewal against the decadent morality and orthodoxy in the state churches of the period. These twin forces of renewal filled the roads leading to some of the more tolerant communities in the Palatinate and Wetterau with pilgrims and refugees. But before we examine these events in detail, let us turn our attention to the general political, economic, and social conditions of German-speaking peoples between 1650 and 1700.

More or less continued warfare marked the period—including wars with France, wars with the Turks, internal wars, and, later, wars with Russia. These were very destructive to villages, farmland, and the populace. Large areas of the Palatinate were rendered all but noninhabitable. The civilian people suffered in indescribable ways from overtaxation, malnutrition, rape, pillage, fire, and disease. Such unfavorable conditions could not help but brutalize and degrade the people in every way. Fear, suspicion, hatred, and superstition were multiplied by other conditions such as arbitrary justice, political tyranny, lack of education, and an unconcerned aristocracy and church leadership.

Moral decay and debauchery were furthered by the upper classes, who imitated the lifestyle of the courts of great kings. Adultery, drunkenness, and sensuality marked the life of the German nobility, with few exceptions. Also, with few exceptions, the clergy of the state churches, enjoying tax protection and official status, turned their heads away from the deplorable lives of the nobility or in hypocrisy gave praise to those in power. Some clergy and church people participated with little restraint in such goings-on themselves. Drunken and immoral clergymen, both Protestant and Catholic, were not uncommon; and many were lazy, worldly, and possessed of little concern for the needs of their spiritual charges. Attendance at church services was compulsory under penalty of some form of discipline.

Because of the wars, many areas of Germany were short of manpower. Trades and occupations were vacant, and the population had greatly declined. This induced some provinces to encourage emigration from other provinces, further increasing the instability and the insecurity of the people. In times of such suffering and deprivation, emotional outlet was taken upon witches, criminals, deviants and religious nonconformists. Horrible tortures, burning, and public punishments were perpetrated against many such unfortunate scapegoats.

Given times such as these, it is understandable that certain sensitive and educated Christians should continue to cry out against immorality and injustice. We should not be surprised, judging from similar protest movements today, that some of the cries were radical and farfetched. Other solutions were cast in more familiar, traditional forms.

Especially significant so far as the impending events at Schwarzenau were concerned was the growth and the influence of Anabaptist ideas. In German provinces, the Anabaptists were excluded from official status and often severely persecuted. Many of them fled to The Netherlands, to Switzerland, and to several towns in the Palatinate and in Wittgenstein, including Schwarzenau. While the ideas of the Anabaptists were familiar to Protestants generally, they were regarded officially by Lutherans and Reformed alike as dangerous, radical, and heretical. The Anabaptists had been organized and cleansed of doctrinal and emotional excesses under the powerful and beneficial leadership of Menno Simons (1492-1559), and many of them were thereafter also called Mennonites.

First among their beliefs was that the Christian life is marked by adult conversion to the faith and adult rebaptism by pouring. Their tendency to rebaptize their followers was a continual source of difficulty with the state churches, who regarded such activities as a repudiation of their own baptism and as proselyting of their members. The Mennonites also denied the alleged lost condition of infants and consequently denied the need for infant baptism. They refused to be drafted to military combat or to take an oath. They were generally obedient to magistrates excepting when such obedience was contrary to the Scriptures or to their consciences. They denied the right of the state to control religion or to force religious adherence. Finally, they practiced feetwashing.

It is important to note that the little group which was baptized in 1708 at Schwarzenau was thoroughly acquainted with Anabaptist and Mennonite views; and the similarity of Brethren belief and practice to theirs is not a matter of mere coincidence. Mack's group, however, espoused other views which set them quite apart from the Mennonites.

The other movement which greatly affected the formation of the Church of the Brethren was Pietism. Pietism may be regarded as a further extension of the Protestant Reformation of the sixteenth century. However, its impact was not primarily at the doctrinal level but at the level of Christian living. The Pietist was one who sought to order his life by the example of Christ as based on the study of the Scriptures.

As favorable as this may sound to the modern-day reader, it should be remembered that the terms *Pietist* and *Anabaptist* were titles of reproach—just as the designations Communist, Socialist, pacifist and so on might represent titles of reproach to many people today.

Pietism incubated in both the Reformed and the Lutheran churches in Germany. It was the Lutheran Church, however, which produced Philip Jacob Spener (1635-1705), who is regarded as its best known leader. In 1675, his little work, *Pious Desires,* which was received with much enthusiasm throughout the country, appealed for improvements in the life of the church. Durnbaugh (1958, page 33)[2] lists the six-point program of improvement called for by Spener: (1) more intensive Bible study, (2) greater participation by laymen in the life and work of the church, (3) Christianity to be seriously practiced in daily life by all, (4) no coercion in religious matters, (5)

---

[2]For convenience, references include only minimal information such as author (if not clear from the narrative), date of the book, and the page number. The precise source may be traced by examining the bibliography, looking under the name of the author, the date of the book, and the page number.

reform in theological training, and (6) more edifying preaching.

While these proposed reforms were regarded as a serious threat to the state churches and the clergy, their reception by the people indicated the widespread sentiment for improvement in the quality of church life. The Bible was still regarded as a book for the learned, and it had not been many years since it was a crime to possess a copy of it. Church life was not run democratically.The hierarchy made decisions, and the heavy hand of the state enforced them. Moral life was at a low ebb. Coercion in religious matters was the established procedure—ranging from changing peoples' religious affiliation to correspond to the religion of the king to compulsory attendance and monetary assessments. In some provinces, religion alternated repeatedly between Lutheran and Reformed in the space of a few dozen years. The cry for better training for clergymen was also heard, because more objective historical writing, rationalism, and advancements in higher scholarship were slow to penetrate the seminaries.

It was August Herman Francke (1663-1727), however, upon whom the mantle of leadership fell and who gave impetus to the Pietistic movement. He was more dynamic and active than was Philip Spener. Because of his work as pastor and teacher in the University of Halle, that German city became the hub of Pietism for all of Europe. Activities such as organizing and running an orphanage, establishing a hospital, and the launching of various social action and study groups took place. Bible study, philanthropic or service programs, and godly living were gradually coming to symbolize a new type of reform emphasis.

At first the Pietists sought merely to change and renew the Protestant churches from within. Many of them never broke with the existing churches at all. Rather, they sought to express their faith by quietly living and witnessing as Lutheran and Reformed Christians.

Other Pietists, however, became disillusioned with the slowness and the difficulties of changing the established churches. These more radical individualists became separated from the established churches. Often their separatism was precipitated by the very church they sought to renew. By virtue of joining small Bible study groups—regarded as illegal and improper by the authorities—they were hounded and harassed until separation was the only alternative to giving up their beliefs. One historian of the period notes that "seldom did the Pietists resolve the break with their churches until that was the only way left to them to stay true to their convictions" (Durnbaugh, 1958, page 37).

On the other hand, some radical Pietists openly proclaimed the necessity of breaking with the established churches and living and worshiping in small, intimate communities or families. These separatists called themselves "the awakened."

One of these more radical separatists was the influential church historian and scholar, Gottfried Arnold (1666-1714), who wrote, according to some views, the first impartial and documented history of the church. Because it was not biased against the Reformers and heretics, it was widely read by the Mennonites and the Pietists and served to fan their convictions concerning the urgency of radical witness.

Gottfried Arnold's writings were well known by the founders of the Church of the Brethren. His book served as an illuminating source pertaining to the nature and the life of the primitive Christian church of the first century. This served as a significant stimulus to Alexander Mack and his associates to practice New Testament, or primitive, Christianity.

It was Ernest Christopher Hochmann von Hochenau (1670-1721), a friend of Gottfried Arnold, however, who completed the quadrangle of leadership which enclosed the Pietistic movement and from which, later, Alexander Mack and his followers departed. Of noble birth and trained at the University of Halle for a promising career in law, Hochmann was awakened to the rightness and the necessity of the godly and simple life of devotion to Christ. He believed that the organized church of his day did not serve as a faithful agent of Christ in calling people to a full Christian experience. Therefore, he devoted his life to an itinerant ministry in Germany, The Netherlands, and Switzerland. Preaching in the homes of the high and the lowly, by his sincerity and pleasant manner he created a powerful following for Pietism. He suffered numerous imprisonments and maltreatments so that his record in this regard is not unlike that of Saint Paul. The Pietism of E. C. Hochmann, G. Arnold, A. Francke and P. Spener had been purged of the excesses of the seventeenth century, and from these men the Brethren founders took much.

Ernest Christopher Hochmann should hold a special place of respect and fondness in the hearts of Brethren. Brumbaugh (1899, page 72) notes that Hochmann and Mack were very close traveling companions in a ministry to the Pietists up and down the Rhine valley. It was under the separate and joint ministries of Mack and Hochmann that most of the men and women who later became Brethren were called out from their "unawakened condition." Hochmann served as an influential guide and spiritual father to the Schwarzenau group during their struggle to decide their course of action. While the precise nature of Mack's indebtedness to Hochmann is in dispute, Mack and the early Brethren differed little from him in major outlook and theology. Primarily they differed only in that Mack was willing to organize a congregation and practice the ordinances as an "outward form." Hochmann believed that this would only lead to heavy persecution and eventually to loss of spiritual content as the ordinances are upheld and practiced only for their own sake. Eventually Mack and Hochmann parted over this issue.

In 1702, Hochmann wrote a short paper, *Confession of Faith*, which served as an unofficial doctrinal guide for the Pietists and the early Brethren alike (Brumbaugh 1899, page 72 ff.). When, in 1708, Mack and his followers finally agreed on the laws and ordinances which were to be practiced in the newly organized fellowship, they were in close conformity with the Hochmann statement except that the exact form for the observance of them (which had not been indicated by Hochmann) was determined—but only after intensive study of the New Testament. In 1715, Mack published his own statement explaining and defending the Brethren beliefs and practices, *The Rights and Ordinances of the House of God*.[3]

---

[3]The original spelling of the first word in the title of Mack's book was "rights." It was changed by Quinter and Kurtz in the 1888 edition (see Durn-

Alexander Mack, Jr., writing in the second preface of his father's book reprinted in its 1799 edition, summarizes the events at the beginning of the eighteenth century. The following quotation is taken from a recent translation of Mack's book.

It pleased the good God in His mercy at the very beginning of this present century and age to support His saving grace, which appears to all men, through some voices calling for repentance and awakening. In this way He awakened many people from the death and sleep of sin. They then sought to find righteousness in Christ. However, they immediately saw to their sorrow great decay almost everywhere. Therefore they felt impelled to give many sincere testimonies of truth about this. Here and there private meetings (in which the newly-awakened souls sought their edification) were established alongside of the usual church organizations. However, because of the spiritual envy of the clergy, the hearts of the authorities were embittered, and persecution began to take place here and there. This happened in Switzerland, the state of Wurttemberg, in the Electoral Palatinate, in the state of Hesse, and many other places. . . .

The Lord then showed these persecuted exiles a place of refuge, or a small Pella, in the county of Wittgenstein. There lived there at that time a lenient count and several awakened countesses. Freedom of conscience was granted at Schwarzenau, about one hour distant from Berleburg. Therefore, although Wittgenstein is a poor and rugged land, many different kinds of people gathered in Schwarzenau. This otherwise little-noticed village was in a short time greatly changed, so that in a few years it was known far and wide. Those who came together there because of persecution were at first called "Pietists," although they differed from one another because of various opinions and also through diverse customs and habits. They themselves, however, called one another "brethren" (Durnbaugh, 1958, pages 37 and 197).

This quotation is historically valuable because it indicates

---

baugh, 1958, page 323). The German word *Rechts* means "laws" or "statutes" in this context.

the sequence of events by which the Pietists, at first devout Lutherans and Reformed Christians, were rejected and excluded by the church and consequently became separatists. Their sins consisted of the holding of Bible study sessions and worship services outside the auspices of the established churches and other intolerable behavior including nonbaptism of their young children, nonoath-taking, nonmilitary service, nonchurch attendance, proselyting, and outspoken criticism of the churches. Because of this, they were forced to flee as refugees to various places. Wittgenstein, a province including Berleburg and Schwarzenau, ruled by kindly and sympathetic Count Henry Albert, became an important Pietistic center to which many, including Alexander Mack, fled. Hochmann himself settled at Schwarzenau, building there a hut which he called *Friedensburg* (Durnbaugh, 1958, page 36). The roads leading into this small village had become crowded with the migrations of the persecuted, and the population increased rapidly.

These Pietists were of course not uniform in either their opinions or their convictions. Most of them were of the Reformed faith. They held to the various Pietist, Anabaptist, and separatist viewpoints in varying degrees, causing one to wonder how they could possibly relate to one another without continual clash of mind. Of course, they had in common a feeling of kinship in their status as refugees and in their expulsion and persecution. While not all of them were ever drawn into any single sectarian movement, be it Brethren, Mennonite, Inspirationist, or what not, the unity which the various groups were able to achieve is due largely to the persuasiveness of their leaders, their consciousness of kind, and their courageous devotion to the ideas which they espoused. At any rate, the situation at Schwarzenau was the kind out of which religious movements are born. But that will be the concern of the next chapter. There we will trace the actual circumstances which brought into existence a struggling but vital and devoted brotherhood.

It has been shown that the impetus for reform and renewal in the church goes far back into the medieval period. The most significant elements of the reform movement arose *within* the church as a concern of those who loved it and were devoted to it. They did not seek to destroy or repudiate the church, but only to bring it closer to the life of Christ.

The reforms in thought and practice were not well received by the established leaders, who perceived danger and threat from those who promoted change. It seemed easier to put down such persons and their ideas. Social scientists today are prone to describe religious institutions as being the most resistant to changes in norms and practices of any of society's institutions. Are these descriptions accurate?

It was noted that in the seventeenth century both Protestant and Catholic churches fought against needed reforms. Those in power appeared to distrust the unauthorized radicals and their unofficial heresies. They did not seem to represent progress or improvement at all. In effect, with some significant exceptions, the leaders did not wish or desire reform.

Today we live in a period of great social unrest and disturbing issues—both doctrinal and social. From all quarters, criticisms and calls for reform are being heard. Many seem radical and threatening. Since freedom of speech and protection of dissenters are legally established in the United States, such radicals are seldom arrested or tortured for expressing their views.

But do Christians today hear any more clearly or understand any more deeply the need for continued growth and renewal within our churches? Do we perceive urgent and needed social changes in race relations, sex roles, and political and economic life as threats and dangers to our comfort and security? Some social critics believe reform will be slow in coming, that present institutions should be completely eradicated and new ones erected in their place. Amidst such a clamor for renewal and change, Christians must avoid two extremes. One is to regard change and modification as evil, as did the established churches of Europe in the seventeenth century and before. The other extreme would be to change too much too rapidly, to discard aspects of faith and practice which are still valid and essential. Our times call for wise and responsible Christian discipline—a discipline of inspired study, prayer, and action.

The study of the reform movements of the past shows that they were generally guided by a practical devotion to the Bible and to humanitarian social concern. While other aspects were present too, it seems appropriate to emphasize these. By stressing the need to be faithful to the Scriptures in doctrine and conduct, the Reformers were in effect lifting up Christ and the early church. Without becoming entangled in either liberalism or legalism, one can see that *the Bible* together with other *literature* and *leadership* which is in harmony with its principles today should and can serve as a source for study and Christian response to pressing social and institutional problems.

The historical account stressed the interrelationship among the various leaders of the Reformation and sectarian movements. These men often knew one another well and were influenced significantly by one another. We saw that Mack and his group were greatly indebted to Pietistic and Anabaptist traditions and that all, in turn, were indebted to the achievements made possible by the Protestant Reformation.

What implications do these interrelationships have for the ecumenical movement today—a movement which has closely touched many Brethren in recent years as our denomination participates in conversations with members of other communions? Can we discover some of the kinship that underlies our common origins in the development of the Protestant Reformation and its various sectarian movements? And what about the deeper kinship that is derived from our service to God and our oneness in Christ?

And, finally, as we follow the intriguing story of the renewal of the church and the events leading up to the baptism in the Eder, can we gain insights concerning the way God pursues his purposes and accomplishes his aims among his people?

2

Founding and Growth in Europe

The object of this chapter is to present a concise review of the organizing and the growth of the Church of the Brethren in Europe up to the time of its migration to America. In the telling of this aspect of Brethren history, it will be possible to stress the contribution of only a few of the leaders of the movement, the circumstances under which they worked, the places involved, and the time elements. Only a minimum of emphasis will be given to the doctrinal and the theological aspects of church formation and growth. Material of this nature will be examined in Chapter 4.

It should be recognized that an attempt to cover in a chapter or two the story of the founding of the church and its growth over two hundred seventy-five years can be only an inadequate and tantalizing recounting of a few major events. However, the reader who is interested in a more detailed account will find that he can go quickly to original sources. The references given and books listed in the chapter will be found in many church libraries or pastors' libraries. If not present there, they may be purchased from The Brethren Press.

The Events Leading up to the Baptism in the Eder

Alexander Mack, regarded as the first "leader," "speaker of the word," and founder of the Church of the Brethren, was born in the summer of 1679 in a small village of southern Germany called Schriesheim. Alexander's father, John Philip

Mack, was a prominent miller and local businessman of middle-class standing and an elder of the Reformed church. For many years, he had been a member of the town council. Durnbaugh (1958, page 52), who gives considerable information about the Mack family, reports that he served as mayor in 1690 and 1696. Before his death in 1706, the elder Mack bequeathed to his two sons, Alexander and John Jacob, considerable wealth, including the mill.

The records of the Reformed Church at Schriesheim reveal the baptism of Alexander Mack on July 27, 1679. On January 18, 1701, Mack was married to Anna Margaret Kling, daughter of a respected townsman and councilor. Five children, three sons and two daughters, were born to the Macks: John Valentine, John, Alexander, Christina, and Anna Maria.[1]

The young Mack family did not remain long in Schriesheim. Both Mack and his wife's family, the Klings, had strong sympathies and leanings toward Pietism. In 1706, Mack invited the famous leader Ernest Christopher Hochmann von Hochenau to come to Schriesheim. A meeting (or series of meetings) to which various citizens of Schriesheim were attracted was held in the Mack mill. Other meetings were held in homes and in the streets. As a result of this disturbing activity and its success in attracting wide interest, the authorities decided to drive the Pietists out. Mack and his wife and young sons escaped to Schwarzenau, but eventually Hochmann was arrested with nine others and sentenced to hard public labor. The Klings were excommunicated from the Reformed Church. Hochmann and two others who were not Palatine subjects were released after a few weeks. The edict of the Elector Palatine, dated September 14, 1706, states:

> It is extremely urgent that this sect—which has an outward hypocritically good appearance, and is therefore much more misleading, but is in itself exceeding dangerous—should be smothered in its first evil brood. . . . Those who

---

[1]For more information concerning Mack and the founding of the church in Germany, see William G. Willoughby, *Counting the Cost: The Life of Alexander Mack,* The Brethren Press, 1979.

commit this evil [to profess Pietism and hold meetings in homes] and who do not respond either to kindly or severe warnings to abandon these wicked intentions and maintain this [their erroneous view] especially stubbornly are to be arrested at once without special authorization. They are to be put in prison, and as many of them as there are must be locked to wheelbarrows and kept on public work on the fortifications and common labor. They are to be separated from one another in various places, and put on a bread-and-water diet. You are to publish this present gracious decree of ours in the entire city so that everyone can conduct himself accordingly and know how to avoid trouble (Durnbaugh, 1958, page 49).

In 1706 and 1707, Mack sold his vineyards and other property. Some of the property, including his interest in the mill, was purchased by his brother, John Jacob. In these and succeeding persecutions, Mack unsparingly used up his considerable wealth in paying the fines of the arrested and in aiding the refugees who had fled to Schwarzenau. It was most likely between the years of 1706 and 1708 that Mack accompanied Hochmann on various missionary journeys in Germany in behalf of Pietism.

Mack, however, was apparently not content with wandering over the countryside with Hochmann. It may be surmised that Mack, having a growing family with several young children, felt the obligations incumbent upon him as a husband and father. Furthermore, Mack and Hochmann did not fully agree on a plan of action. Hochmann was one of the more extreme German separatists. He did not accept the necessity for religious organization, clergy, sacraments, and anything else that reminded him of the outward expressions of churchness. He was interested only in a spiritual church having no ritual, sacraments, or buildings. Mack never fully shared these views. It is possible that in the two years between his leaving Schriesheim and the baptism in the Eder he gave serious consideration to the extreme separatist position. But he decided forthrightly against it. More urgently than Hochmann, Mack felt the need to be obedient to all biblical commands.

One of the deep concerns felt by Mack and a few other

Pietists who had sought refuge in Wittgenstein was for their unbaptized state. While they had repudiated infant baptism and some of them had been excommunicated, they fully believed and accepted the Bible. Their study of the New Testament seemed to indicate the existence of an organized church in the first century and the practice of certain rites such as baptism, anointing, and the Lord's Supper. Full obedience to the Bible seemed to involve the need for practicing these rites and the creation of simple organization if the commandments of the New Testament were to be fullfilled.

Consequently, Mack, his wife, and six others, in the year 1708, entered into intensive and prolonged prayer and study to determine what was involved in full obedience to Christ and the New Testament. Mack continued his correspondence with Hochmann, who was at the time in prison in Nuernberg. Hochmann replied to Grebe and Mack in a letter dated July 24, 1708 (Durnbaugh, 1958, pages 110-115) that he would not permit himself to be against adult baptism since Christ had allowed himself to be baptized. But he was not convinced that the need for baptism was really a conviction from God. He indicated that he believed that nothing but the cross and misery would result from rebaptism. He saw that it would engender opposition and persecution from the state churches. He warned that the Schwarzenau group should carefully "count the cost" before following these outward forms. He gently reminded them also that God does not look on the outside, but rather on the inward condition of the heart. Included in the thoughtful and brotherly letter from Hochmann was the concern that outward forms would not degenerate into empty legalistic practices without spiritual content. Undoubtedly, Mack and the rest were as fully aware as Hochmann of these dangers, but none could possible foretell exactly how and when the future would reveal these dangers and threats of which they spoke.

It was sometime late in the summer of 1708 that the first eight determined to become fully obedient to the imperatives of the New Testament. They accepted upon themselves what they fully believed to be the commandments of Christ. Knowingly, they were accepting also the inevitable consequences

which this unreserved obedience was to bring. It was a part of
the price to be paid for discipleship. At the time of this decision
it was concluded that a written statement should be circulated
among the Pietists explaining their plans. It is not known who
prepared this open letter since the author was chosen by lot.
Durnbaugh (1958, page 115), who has translated and published
this document for the first time, rightly stresses the fact that
its tone is one of faithful obedience to God and his Word. An
urgent invitation was also extended to like-minded Pietists to
join in the baptism to which the first eight were called. The attitude and the concern of this letter are well worth thoughtful
study today. In it one can discern a genuine Christian spirit,
faithful devotion to God, and a courageous acceptance of that
which is believed to be right whatever the cost.

Durnbaugh estimates from a study of the sequence of
events as they are recorded in the archives in Germany that
the baptism took place between early August and late
September. Five men and three women participated in the
historic occasion.[2] A person chosen by lot first baptized Alexander Mack, who in turn baptized the rest. That their baptism
did not stand directly in the apostolic succession was of no
great concern to them. Baptism was not regarded as in itself
being the instrument of salvation. It was merely symbolic of
their total commitment to Christ and of God's salvation
granted them through his grace.

Growth in Germany

Living as we do in a period of great religious freedom and
toleration of sectarian practices, it is difficult for us to con-
ceive of the radical nature of that first Brethren baptism. This
and subsequent baptismal rites were the subject of endless
gossip and rumor in Schwarzenau and nearby Berleberg. The
event was not unnoticed by the political authorities, some of
whom were greatly incensed. They regarded this "Anabaptist

---

[2]The names of the first eight members were: Alexander Mack of
Schriesheim, George Grebe and Luke Vetter from Hesse, Andrew Boni from
Basel, John Kipping from Bareit, Joanna Nothiger (or Boni), Anna Mack, and
Joanna Kipping.

sect" as a severe threat to law and order in the province. Religious authorities saw in these immersions a wicked repudiation of infant baptism and interpreted them to be a direct attack upon the church.

Henry Albert, ruler of Wittgenstein and friend of Alexander Mack, sought to continue his policy of broad toleration of the Pietists and the Anabaptists. He was viciously attacked, however, by his brother-in-law, Count Charles Louis of Sayn-Wittgenstein, for his permissiveness toward Mack and the "New Baptists" (Neu-Taufer) or Taüfgesinnte, as they were sometimes called. In 1709-1710, Charles Louis fired off a battery of letters to various authorities concerning the alleged disgraceful situation. These letters, translated and published by Durnbaugh, offer a fascinating running account both of Brethren developments and of the reactions of the authorities to Brethren activities. Mack and his followers are described in the lowest terms as evil, criminal, and immoral rabble rousers whose continued activity brings ill fame to all the noble families. Their extermination by sword and fire is called for in intemperate words. Mack is specifically accused of not allowing his children to be baptized and of persuading adults to be rebaptized.

Schwarzenau and nearby Berleberg had become well-known centers of tolerance. In 1708, these two villages contained perhaps some five or six hundred refugees. They comprised a convenient but not necessarily receptive audience for the views of the new group. Nevertheless, conversions into the newly organized sect must have come rather frequently. Several letters written in 1709 by Count Charles Louis not only illustrate the favorable response of the refugees of Wittgenstein to the preaching of Mack and his fellow Brethren but also show the increasing concern of the authorities over their growth. While the actual number of converts in Schwarzenau and Berleberg is not known, a strong community was undoubtedly built up during the succeeding seven years. Mallott (1954, page 37) reports that Schwarzenau became the largest congregation of Brethren on the European continent.

Mack, Jr., wrote of this period of growth in the church in the preface of his father's small book indicating that by 1715 a large congregation existed in Schwarzenau. He also indicated that during those seven years powerful witnesses were called to the service of the Lord in Schwarzenau and Marienborn. Their names were John Kalkleser of Frankenthal, Christian Liebe and Abraham Duboy of Epstein, John Naas of Nordheim, and Peter Becker of Dillsheim. Other leaders were John Trout, Henry Holsopple, Stephen Koch, George B. Gansz, and Michael Eckerlin. All eventually became ministers in the church. These men were full of zeal and sought to propagate the faith to which they had committed themselves. Persecutions in Schwarzenau did not prevent the growth and spread of the new fraternity. Many converts were forced to flee to other places of refuge. In 1715, after severe persecutions in Marienborn, the new fellowship there moved to Krefeld. An additional congregation was established in Epstein. Besides this, individual Brethren were living in other places in Germany and also in Switzerland. All of this growth took place in the space of eleven years, between 1708 and the first migration to the New World in 1719.

Missionary Activities, Persecution, and Perseverance

In recent years, many previously unknown records of Brethren activity in Germany have come to light. Much of this new knowledge has come as a result of the research of Professor Durnbaugh of Bethany Theological Seminary. Other fragments of information have been known for many years. Some of these events and stories tell of precious aspects of Brethren heritage and ought to be widely known by contemporary Brethren.

Some of these happenings, of course, center around the life of Mack. It has already been noted that Mack inherited considerable wealth from his father. Because of his compassion, this wealth was completely expended in ministering to the common good of the impoverished converts and in payment of their fines during periods of persecutions. It is recorded that in the end he himself was penniless because of his generosity and brotherly deeds though he was not poor in spirit.

The years in Germany were marked by missionary activity, often conducted at great personal risk by Brethren leaders who took the scriptural command of Matthew 28:19-20 quite literally. A series of documents stored at Buedingen tell the remarkable story of Mack's evangelistic ministry at Marienborn. This village was under the rule of Count Ernest Casimer, who in an edict published in 1712 assured relgious toleration to various craftsmen and artisans who would come there to work and live. He thereby hoped to strengthen the rundown economy. Many Pietists settled there, and among them were several Schwarzenau Brethren who soon developed a brotherhood. Because of this, Mack frequently went there to preach and conduct the Lord's Supper and baptism.

These public religious services were regarded as dangerous by the count, in spite of his edict of toleration. In August 1711, Alexander Mack visited Marienborn, staying with Jacob Bossert. On the twenty-first of the month, a service was held in which the daughter of Eva Elizabeth Hoffman was baptized. As a result of this disturbance of the peace, Mrs. Hoffman was ordered expelled from the province and Mack was forbidden to return. Villagers were warned not to extend hospitality to him under penalty of severe punishment.

Not to be restrained from being obedient to the command of Christ to preach and baptize, Mack came twice more to Marienborn and conducted the rite. In November 1712, he baptized four persons, including the wife of John Naas. This time the authorities, fully aware of the honesty of Mack and also of the Brethren refusal to swear, obliged him before he could be released to promise with a handshake that he would never return. True to his promise, Mack remained away.

A fourth baptism, that of Peter Becker and his wife, was conducted in May 1714 by John Naas. Becker, who was to become an important leader, and his wife were subjects of the count and not refugees. Partly because of this and partly because of the growth of the Inspirationists, who also were regarded as troublemakers, the authorities decided on more drastic measures. The Brethren hereafter were to limit their services to devotions in their homes. If they did not agree to this, they were to be expelled from the province. They decided to migrate as a group to Krefeld, and in May 1715 they received a passport from the count with his warm recommendation to whoever would receive them.

Krefeld and Solingen, along the lower Rhine, were famous as places of refuge for persecuted sectarians. The Mennonites were especially numerous in the region—and also especially hospitable to the Brethren. The Brethren in the lower Rhine area had strong and able leadership in the persons of Peter Becker, John Naas, and Christian Liebe. Both Mennonites and Reformed Church people were attracted.

A baptism of six men and several women was held in Solingen in 1717. Harsh reprisals were taken against them, and the six Brethren were arrested in February 1717 and sentenced to imprisonment at hard labor for life. Fortunately, the sentence was annulled after four years because of the intervention of many persons on their behalf.

In 1763, one of the men, William Grahe, wrote a complete and detailed account of the entire experience. It became a famous document and was frequently read throughout Germany as a lesson in faithfulness to Christ. Durnbaugh (1958, pages 241-268) has published Grahe's remarkable story in full. It represents as courageous an account of endurance and loving devotion to God under trying circumstances as one is likely to find. The persecution of Christian Liebe is well-known but bears repeating here—if for no other reason than to remind modern Brethren in a time of religious freedom of the price of faithfulness which was paid by our spiritual forebears. Would our religious life be deeper and stronger if we were required to suffer for it?

Liebe, who was at the time a resident of the Palatinate, had made a trip in 1714 to Bern, Switzerland, to minister to Brethren there. The timing of Liebe's visit was inauspicious since the Bern city council was involved in an active suppression of Anabaptists. Liebe admitted that his purpose was to minister, to give comfort, and to baptize—even though these activities were expressly forbidden. The council decided to make an example of Liebe and some other Anabaptist ministers by sentencing them to life imprisonment on the galleys. Subsequently, they were kept in a prison with ninety other criminals through the winter until it became feasible to transport them to a ship flying the flag of Sicily. Finally, after a harrowing ordeal lasting two years, in which two of the five ministers died, Liebe and the others were released. The account of the arrangements for release are remarkable in showing the sympathetic intervention on the part of Mennonites, Swiss nobility, and the Dutch government.

The life of John Naas is unusual in several respects. He was a man of great physical strength and power. His leadership is well-attested by the *Chronicon Ephratense* (the *Ephrata Chronicle*, an account written about half a century later at the Ephrata Cloisters, Pennsylvania), which described him as the "incomparable teacher." His ministry at Marienborn and Krefeld was one which tended to soften the impact of creeping legalism.

Naas himself did not escape persecution. Recruiting officers of the Prussian king, in search of men suitable for combat training, greatly desired Naas because of his unusual height and outstanding physique. But Naas, true to the command "Thou shalt not kill," refused military service. The king's officers sought to compel him through torture to change his mind. The torture consisted of pinching, thumb-screwing, and finally hanging by the right great toe and left thumb (see Brumbaugh, 1899, pages 100-130). Despite these humiliating and painful treatments he remained faithful, and the officers cut him down fearing his death. He was finally dragged before the king, to whom he explained that his first service was to the Prince of Peace. The king, admiring Naas's great courage and perseverance, commended him and released him with the gift of a gold coin.

Other outstanding leaders served the church in Europe, but information concerning their work is not abundant. These persons—Stephen Koch, Abraham Duboy, John H. Kalkleser, John Hildebrand, Andreas Frey, and Peter Becker—deserve special mention. Brumbaugh (1899) and others have written concerning their lives and work. Their lives deserve more study by Brethren today than they have received. They comprise a vital part of the rich heritage of our church. Their lives are a source of inspiration and faithfulness to all those who are exposed to them.

Migration from Krefeld

The Brethren groups at Krefeld and Solingen grew rapidly in fame though not rapidly in numbers. Interest was stirred among the Pietists, the Reformed, and the Mennonites. Prospects for growth were good. Following his release from the galleys, Christian Liebe, a persuasive speaker of great popularity, came to Krefeld as one of the leaders, serving under Elder Naas. In 1719 or before, great sadness and tragedy befell the growing fellowship, serving as a good illustration of how an intolerant attitude and unforgiving spirit can disrupt the well-being of a congregation. Naas and Liebe did not agree and could not work together. The reasons for this are not fully known. The *Ephrata Chronicle* (pages 3, 248-249), not sympathetic toward the Brethren, describes the conflict; but it is tantalizingly brief.

It appears that a young minister, Hacker by name, married a woman who had not been baptized. Undoubtedly, Hacker's mistake was in marrying out of the church. The *Chronicle,* however, suggests that some in the church may have desired to punish him also for his violation of the norm of celibacy (1 Corinthians 7). At any rate, disagreement among the ministers had serious consequences. Naas, more moderate in his reaction, had the support of the congregation in merely suspending Hacker from participating in communion. Liebe and four other celibates reacted more harshly and placed Hacker under the ban, nearly equivalent to excommunication.

The *Chronicle* (page 249) indicates that because of this schism some one hundred persons who had been convinced of the need for rebaptism were turned away. Discouraged and perhaps believing that his retirement would benefit the congregation, Naas, the senior minister, moved away to Switzerland, leaving the fellowship under the care of Liebe and the other ministers. The congregation was unresponsive to Liebe, and he became embittered. The work fell into the hands of Peter Becker, whose quiet but effective ministry brought partial healing. In 1719, perhaps partly because of the schism, a small group of families, under the leadership of Peter Becker, sailed for Pennsylvania.

It is impossible to know all the reasons why the Krefeld

Brethren chose Pennsylvania as their new home. The fact that William Penn had established a sanctuary in which religious refugees from Europe could be assured of religious freedom was surely not unknown to the Brethren. Perhaps even more influential, however, was the close relation of the Brethren with the Mennonites in the Krefeld area. This had long been a Mennonite settlement. A number of Mennonite emigrations to Pennsylvania had already taken place. Correspondence from these emigrants kept the Krefeld sectarians well informed of opportunities and attractions in the colonies. In view of the favorable reputation of Penn's state and the success of the Mennonites who had already made the voyage, it was plausible for the Becker group to settle there.

Migration from Schwarzenau

Around 1720, the Schwarzenau Brethren under the leadership of Alexander Mack moved to Surhuisterveen in West Friesland in The Netherlands. Increased persecution is sometimes given as the reason for this move. On the other hand, Durnbaugh (1958, page 289) points out that Henry Albert's policy of toleration was maintained until 1723. Difficulties with the Inspirationists, the need for religious freedom, and economic problems likely entered into the causes of the move. The land in the Wittgenstein area was of poor quality. At any rate, West Friesland was their home between 1720 and 1729. During these years some of them were employed cutting peat moss in the marshy areas being drained and in following their trades as artisans.

An interesting record concerning the removal of Mack and his group from Schwarzenau has been preserved in Germany. It consists of a letter written by one of Count Henry's officials, Frederick Christian Lade, in Schwarzenau, supplying information to the imperial solicitor at Wetzlar, who was conducting an investigation of religious conditions in the province. It contains a paragraph which may be taken as an official description of the character of the Brethren in Schwarzenau.

I therefore report in obedient compliance to his request that many pious people resided here for a time, about whom

one heard nothing evil, but rather perceived they they conducted themselves quietly and devoutly in all things. No person has ever complained about them. From this group, forty
families, numbering about two hundred persons, recently
left this country permanently (Durnbaugh, 1958, page 291).

Finally, in 1729, the Mack group of around one hundred
twenty left Rotterdam aboard the *Allen* for Philadelphia. The
voyage lasted from July 7 to September 11. So far as is known,
no organized congregation remained in Europe for long after
1729. Naas, who had moved to Switzerland, and presumably
settled among the Brethren there, came to Pennsylvania in
1733.[3] A few Brethren remained in Solingen, but they gradually affiliated with the Mennonites. Perhaps subsequent
research in Europe will uncover further information about
Brethren remnants there.

Epilogue on the Brethren in Europe

The emigrations in 1729 and 1733 bring to a close the
story of the Brethren founding and expansion in Europe.
Before leaving this topic, however, it may be of value to review
the European period, the years from 1708 to 1733.

There is no way of knowing accurately the strength of the
Brethren in Europe. Of the two main congregations,
Schwarzenau was probably the larger. An official document
dated June 24, 1720 (Durnbaugh, 1958, page 291), reported the
size of the migrating portion of the Schwarzenau congregation
at forty families, around two hundred persons. In this migration to West Friesland some members may have been left
behind and been lost to the Brotherhood. This was certainly
the case in the lower Rhine area. Only a few Brethren from
other scattered areas in Germany and Switzerland are known
to have emigrated to the British North American colonies. The
Mack group emigrated from West Friesland in 1729. Mallott

---

[3]John Naas wrote a moving and tragic description of his voyage in 1733.
It illuminates the difficulties of transoceanic voyages during this time. For
the account, refer to Brumbaugh, 1899, pages 108-124, and Durnbaugh, 1958,
pages 302-312.

(1954, page 40), after studying the *Allen's* passenger list, believes that the group consisted of fifty-seven families with only five children under fifteen. The men and the women were about equal in number, and the total number was likely between one hundred fifteen and one hundred twenty. The size of the families was small. It is not known whether this was due to celibate tendencies or the tendency for only the older couples and families without children to emigrate. Perhaps not all the children were included in the ship's list. It is known that transoceanic mortality rates were very high, especially for children.[4]

Records of the Becker emigration are less complete and are therefore problematic. Brumbaugh (1899, pages 49, 52), basing his information on a misused quotation from Goebel, is undoubtedly wrong in describing the group as consisting of forty families and two hundred persons. Mallot (1954, page 39), probably relying on Brumbaugh, also indicates that forty families accompanied Becker. Actually, the group must have been smaller. The *Ephrata Chronicle* (pages 3 and 249) reports only that "a party" or "several others" moved with Becker to America. Morgan Edwards (Durnbaugh, 1967, page 173) indicates that about twenty families came in this group. It is difficult to know with what reliability to regard the Edwards figure, which was written down in 1770. Presumably his information is derived from contemporary Brethren.

Another valuable source of information concerning the numerical strength of the Brethren is Martin G. Brumbaugh's list of two hundred twenty-five names of persons who were believed to be affiliated with the church in Europe. Many of these people did not emigrate to America. There is no way of knowing how nearly complete or how inconclusive this list is. It would not be surprising if many names of converts were omitted.

The growth in Europe would appear remarkable for a period as short as twenty years. This is so because of the condi-

---

[4]For information on shipboard deaths, see Durnbaugh, 1967, pages 48-53. An interesting and informative fictional story of the experiences of the Becker-led group is Roy White's *Stormy Crossing* (Elgin: Brethren Press, 1963).

tions of disfavor and persecution, repeated uprootings, and opposition from established churches. Natural increase by reproduction was not a likely source of growth during this period. The phenomenal increase which did take place undoubtedly was due to intensive evangelistic zeal and activity. That the church would grow under such adverse conditions as persecution and active suppression speaks both to the quality of the spiritual character of our founders and to the depth of their commitment.

This lesson could be taken to heart by Brethren today whose denominational growth rate for the past three decades has certainly been less than spectacular. Our heritage as Brethren is great. Our calling from Christ is worthy. The world is in need of the message of the Prince of Peace. Therefore, our witness must be more enthusiastic and our commitment much deeper!

Establishment and Growth in America

Development in Pennsylvania

The arrival in Pennsylvania of the small group of twenty or so families of the Krefeld Brethren with Peter Becker in 1719 did not result in the immediate establishment of an organized church. This had to wait until the passing of four years, until the end of 1723. What were the conditions which the new immigrants faced upon their arrival in 1719? Particularly, what kinds of problems and situations had a bearing upon the delay in organized religious activity which apparently followed their arrival and then which related to the renewal of religious fervor among them after a few years?

The religious dissension which was engendered by the Hacker incident in Krefeld is usually given as the main reason for the slowness of the immigrants to organize in Pennsylvania. The *Ephrata Chronicle* and later historians who relied upon this source have tended to stress this factor. Undoubtedly, any hidden or open disagreement or disharmony might have been greatly enhanced by the horrible conditions of prolonged confinement of the six- to twelve-week voyage. (See *Stormy Crossing.*) Even families and spouses sometimes were alienated by this experience.

Without minimizing the effect of this factor, it should be recognized that other causes also made it quite difficult if not impossible for the fellowship immediately to resume the effective functioning it had had in Krefeld. For one thing, the families did not all settle in the same vicinity. Some were separated by many miles with no ready means of travel. A small nucleus, including Becker, settled at Germantown. Other families settled as far away as Skippack, the Schuylkill region, Oley, and Falckner's Swamp. There is no certain evidence that the Germantown nucleus did not quickly resume religious meetings, but it was several years until those whose search for land had led them to more distant places could come together to worship.

The harsh conditions under which the struggle for survival in the wilderness took place must not be overlooked. Immediate and urgent problems needed to be solved. Houses had to be built. Trades had to be resumed and clients secured. Heavy timber had to be cleared and rocks had to be piled before the first crop could be planted. The building of a farm out of the raw Pennsylvania wilderness was a project requiring backbreaking effort over a period of years.

While economic conditions were undoubtedly hard, especially at first, there was a new element in the economic activity of the Brethren immigrant, something entirely absent in the lives of these humble poor in Germany. They were developing their own farms. Landowning was a totally new experience to most of them. Here the possibility of owning many hundreds of acres and one's own house was a new motivation. Hard work and perseverance—traits well ingrained by their European background—held promise here of sure personal benefit and even wealth unthought of in their homeland. Land was cheap, advertised by Penn at one hundred acres for forty shillings. Indeed, if we judged by the critical remarks of the rival sect of Seventh Day Baptists under Beissel, many Brethren were succumbing to the ambition to accumulate land and wealth. Certainly, an adjustment to totally new and radically different economic conditions was required to the Brethren immigrant. Economically, the church in America was moving in a direction entirely different from that of the period of communal sharing under Mack's leadership in Schwarzenau. The presence of a materialistic and economic motivation among the Brethren has continued to the present. Perhaps now this motivation is to be consecrated to Christ rather than to be denied and uprooted.

The struggles and difficulties present in the new environment did not extinguish the deeply rooted religious devotion and commitment of the Brethren. The urgent problems of survival and establishment had taken a necessary priority over merely formal religious activities for a time. At Germantown, under the leadership of Becker, religious fervor was evident. It is possible that religious meetings were maintained from the beginning among the Brethren in the vicinity of Germantown (Blough, *History of the Church of the Brethren in Eastern Pennsylvania*, 1915, page 17). At any rate, in the fall of 1722 five Germantown men, including Becker, made a trip to visit the scattered families and hold services in their homes. This work was fruitful and a sense of unity and eagerness was stimulated. The following year a coming together of some of the scattered families at Germantown resulted in the holding of a love feast and a baptismal service on Christmas Day. Traditionally, this date, December 25, 1723, has been regarded as the formal beginning of the first congregation of the Church of the Brethren in the New World. Brumbaugh (1899, pages 155-160), relying on the information given in the *Chronicle* (pages 22ff.), has described the remarkable events of this day in great detail and with a considerable degree of nostalgia. However they are described, there is no doubt that this day signaled an encouraging revival of the old conviction and missionary enthusiasm which was very pronounced among the membership in Germany.

Meetings continued and a "great awakening" began the following spring in the Germantown area. No houses were capable of accommodating the crowds. The young people as well as their elders were drawn into the tides of emotion and religious sentiment. It was decided to carry the revival into the outlying areas. Meetings and communions were held during the summer, and the *Chronicle* (page 23) reports that their fellowship experienced a rapid growth. During October and November of 1724, Peter Becker and thirteen others from Germantown visited several of the outlying settlements, including Falckner's Swamp, Oley, and the Schuylkill region. At the latter place, on November 7, communion and baptism were held and an organization was formed with Martin Urner being elected to the ministry. This is the record of the formation of Coventry, the second congregation in America. The total beginning membership there consisted of nine persons.

On November 12, meetings were held at the house of Henry Hohn at Conestoga, and seven persons were baptized. This number included Conrad Beissel, an ascetic-minded celibate who soon separated from the Brethren to found the Seventh Day Baptist Community at Ephrata. Beissel was exceedingly mystical and fervent, and because of his divisive and proselyting work he attracted some of the Brethren into his movement over the succeeding fifteen or twenty years. On November 19, another meeting and a baptismal service were held, and Beissel was elected as a minister. Conestoga is the third congregation of the Church of the Brethren in the New World.

The Beissel division brought great sorrow to the early church. Beissel's tendencies toward monasticism, celibacy, and Sabbatarianism—together with his extreme individualism and exaggerated sense of self-importance—prevented him from working with the Brethren. The Conestoga church, and finally between 1735 and 1740 the Germantown church, were struck with division and conflict. A total of seventeen adults, including two sons and a daughter of Alexander Mack, were among Beissel's converts. Other gifted leaders joined with Beissel in building an astonishingly prosperous and entirely unique monastic community in America. Its remnants still exist in the form of remarkably well-preserved buildings near Ephrata and ·Waynesboro. The complex of structures near Ephrata has now been taken as a monument by the Pennsylvania Historical and Museum Commission. During the time of its greatest prosperity this monastic community operated an influential printing press and produced literature and music whose fame reached over the colonies and even back to Germany. While the Ephrata movement was never a part of the Church of the Brethren, its history during its first fifty years in America is intimately entwined with that of the Brethren and can scarcely be ignored in any serious historical treatment.

Without exception, the tendency of all of the Brethren was

to hold their religious services in their homes. Although a total of at least sixteen congregations had been organized in Maryland, New Jersey, and Pennsylvania by 1770, no church houses had been built except in the urbanizing congregation at Germantown, whose plain and small "meetinghouse" was constructed in that year. The Brethren rotated their meetings from home to home (sometimes in barns) among those members whose houses were large enough to accommodate the gatherings. Later these houses were especially constructed with movable partitions. Yet today these sturdy, well-built homes may be found from Pennsylvania to Virginia and to the West as far as Ohio and Indiana.[1]

Floyd Mallott (1954, page 61) reminds us that the early Brethren, by meeting in homes, were clearly imitating the "primitive Christians" of the New Testament period and expressing their reluctance to become like the prideful, worldly, and highly organized churches against whom the European Pietists had reacted. It is illuminating to note how a gradual and scarcely perceptible evolution in attitudes has taken the church in two hundred seventy-five years so far from the ideals of the founders. Without concluding that it is desirable to have all our doctrines remain unchanged, we can see that this points up the necessity for continually being on guard against the modification or the loss of any of our doctrines which we now prize as "eternal verities." On the other hand, perhaps all the doctrines and practices of the church must be discovered, adopted, and applied by each generation to its own life.

In 1729, the Mack group arrived from West Friesland. Their numbers—around one hundred fifteen to one hundred twenty—served greatly to augment the young church in Pennsylvania. Some of the immigrants remained in the territory of the mother church. Others scattered into the wilderness and affiliated themselves with the already-established Brethren

---

[1]In 1968, for example, the old Yount home, built in Broadway, Virginia, around 1800, has been renovated by Reverend and Mrs. Samuel Lindsay. This house was used for many years as a meeting place. It contains a large room which, when the hinged partition is opened, provides an area eighteen by thirty-five feet in size.

communities. In 1733, John Naas and several others arrived and settled in New Jersey, forming the Amwell congregation in that year. Also, about this time two new congregations were formed in Berks County: Oley and Great Swamp.

Mack was greatly beloved by the Brethren, and his leadership was respected and desired. His settlement at Germantown strengthened that group at a time when the Beissel controversy was raging. Unfortunately, the struggling young churches were not to have the blessing of his ministry for long. His death in 1735 brought great sorrow to all. The funeral of Mack has been described imaginatively and in sad detail by Freeman Ankrum (1943, pages 6-11). The Germantown church could ill afford to lose the cohesive and binding ministry of its founder-leader. In search of the mystical and emotional experience associated with their original awakening, many good members abandoned the mother church to hold with Beissel, some returning later in disappointment and remorse.

Growth and Spread of the Brethren to 1790

These troubles did not prevent the churches from growing in size, increasing in number, and generally prospering. The causes of growth were of several kinds. Pioneer families tended to be large, and natural increase was certainly a primary factor in growth. A significant proportion of baptisms in the succeeding generations of the church tended to be of the offspring of the Brethren families. In addition, preaching and continued missionary activity, especially among the German-speaking peoples and the new immigrants, proved effective. There was present already a strong consciousness of kind and a sense of affinity due to common language and German cultural background. The number of German-speaking peoples was continually being increased because of immigration.

Another factor in the growth of the church was the tendency of the members to establish new communities and attract other Germans into their religious fellowship. The sturdy pioneers were strongly attracted to the new and unopened lands in western Pennsylvania, Maryland, and Virginia. Whenever Brethren families moved, they attempted to settle close enough together that they could continue their social and religious ties. After having established themselves in new lands, they would communicate with Brethren back at the home settlements, encouraging them to come. In this way, more distant communities of Brethren were established at Stony Creek, Bedford County, Pennsylvania; Antietam and Conococheague along the Maryland-Pennsylvania line; Middletown Valley, Monocacy, and Pipe Creek in Maryland; Beaver Run in what is now West Virginia; and in the Shenandoah Valley of Virginia, by 1790. Continued zealous preaching in these many new communities, often without strong churches of other denominations, continually increased their number.

The famous Baptist historian, Morgan Edwards, in 1770 listed fourteen Brethren (or Dunker) churches in Pennsylvania, one in New Jersey, seven in Maryland, and seven in Virginia and the Carolinas. While it is difficult today to identify with certainty all of the Southern churches he referred to, his records were fairly accurate and reliable. In addition to merely naming the Pennsylvania and Maryland churches, he also named their ministers and often listed the names of the members and the total membership of the churches (Durnbaugh, 1967, pages 173-191). At the time of Edwards' writing in 1770, there were 419 families, 763 baptized persons, and an estimated total (five persons to a family) of 2,095 individuals in the Pennsylvania churches. To this may be added the forty-six members listed by Edwards at Amwell and the members of the Maryland churches, of which there were 462. Edwards lists thirty-six members in Virginia and 208 in the six Carolina churches. Thus, the total membership of all the churches according to these records would be 1,515 at the time when the young denomination was only sixty-two years of age.

Travel was tedious and dangerous in the period before 1790. Major trails to the West had not yet carried large numbers of pioneer wagons. It is estimated that only five percent of the American population of under four million lived west of the Allegheny Mountains. The river valleys which ran predominantly northward and southward just east of the highest Appalachian range served to channel migrants and provided tempting places to settle. At least six congregations with a total membership of 368 were located in the valleys drained by the tributaries of the Potomac in 1770. By 1785, another growing congregation, Beaver Run, was established on tributaries of the Potomac in Hampshire County, Virginia (now West Virginia). The lost church of the South Branch, under the leadership of the Powers family, had been founded by this time. Queries from this congregation were considered by the Annual Conferences of 1785 and 1790, but extended historical references to this church are unknown (Bittinger, 1945, page 32).

The most frequent routes southward followed the Monacacy River to Frederick, Maryland, crossed the South (Braddock) Mountain, wound through the narrow confines of the gap of the Potomac River at Harper's Ferry, and entered the Shenandoah Valley near Winchester. Braddock's Road opened up the area beyond the Appalachian ranges in western Pennsylvania.

Wherever the thrifty and hardworking German sectarians settled, there appeared not only the rough cabins surrounded by the newly planted fields cleared out of the primeval forests but also the large families of children which constituted the potential resource for a spiritual harvest in the expanding membership. Where these families laid the foundations for their houses they also planted the foundations for the house of God. The church was in their houses and in their hearts. There was no mistaking them for non-Christians. Unlike many of their modern counterparts, because of their plain dress and religious way of life they were neither unrecognized nor anonymous in their communities. Their relations to the household of faith and the presence of a congregation were important factors in deciding where to settle and how far away to set up a new household. The early Brethren were certainly geographically mobile. It would be useful to know just how much value was placed upon religious and kinship ties as compared with other factors when decisions to move were made. One wishes that it were possible to compare today's families with those of yesteryear with respect to the factors which induce them to move. Are religious and family considerations less important to the Brethren now than they were then?

At the same time that the church was increasing through

migration and dispersion to the south and the west it was also putting down roots in the fertile soil of Pennsylvania. Conestoga is an amazing example. Royer has given us an excellent account of the development of this local fraternity, including the effect of dispersion and migration to the year 1908.

> Conestoga was one of the first organized colonial churches. In 1730, it had about thirty-five communicants. In 1748, it had 200; in 1770, having by that time received over 400 into fellowship it had only 86 communicants. From the very beginning, Conestoga church was now weakened by emigration, then recruited and strengthened by the faithful, earnest application of the home-community missionary method.
>
> In 1846, the Annual Meeting was held in the reduced territory then known as the Conestoga church. But the Conestoga of '46 is today seven congregations with a membership of over 1600. Growth—growth by the home community missionary method (Royer in *Two Centuries of the Church of the Brethren,* page 78).

The development of the Conestoga church is further pictured by Mallott (1954, pages 71-72).

> The Conestoga brotherhood numbered about twenty when Michael Frantz took charge, and it had increased to about two hundred at his death. The church had the good fortune to have a worthy successor to Michael Frantz in the person of Michael Pfautz. He presided over the congregation from a few weeks after his ordination, September 25, 1748, until his death on May 14, 1769. The congregation grew surprisingly. In the first year of his eldership, fifty-seven persons were added to the church. From 1749 to 1755, one hundred more were baptized. The story goes that there were then seven years of barrenness, followed by another fruitful period. We are not sure whether Jacob Sontag or Christian Longenecker succeeded Michael Pfautz immediately, but soon after 1770 it was Elder Longenecker.
>
> One of the very valuable evidences of research in Brumbaugh's history is his listing of the names of four hundred sixty-three persons who joined the Conestoga

church from the days of Michael Frantz to the year 1799.
In 1770, there were only fifty-three families and eighty-
six persons on the communion roll. But that is eloquent
testimony to the influence of Conestoga. The members
had migrated south and west, and they carried their faith
with them.

Further description by Royer is illuminating:

> What can we say for colonial Conestoga today? For we
> still have her with us. Her territory has been divided and
> sub-divided until there are now within her original boundary
> twenty congregations with a total membership of nearly
> 5,000 souls (in *Two Centuries of the Church of the Brethren*,
> page 78).

The continued growth of the church during the next period
of its history is a further elaboration on these two themes: (1)
strengthening and enlargement of the older churches by
natural increase, evangelizing, and subdividing; and (2)
establishment of new congregations in distant places as a
result of migration.

Growth During the Nineteenth Century

In 1790, the population center of the United States was
east of Baltimore, and one-half of the people of this young nation lived on the Atlantic side of that point. The Brethren arriving in 1719 were comparative latecomers to the continent.
At the time the Brethren arrived, the lands of eastern and central Pennsylvania were just being opened up. Following the
Revolutionary War, vast new lands west of the Appalachians
were waiting to be settled. The period of massive westward
migration was about to get under way. In the one hundred
years from 1790 to 1890, the population center of the United
States shifted westward from east of Baltimore to a point adja-
cent to the eastern edge of Ohio in 1840 and then to a point
within Indiana in 1890, a distance of over five hundred miles.
In a figurative, if not a precisely accurate sense, the population
of the country was going west.

The Brethren were an integral part of this migration. Indeed, they were on the forefront since their settlements had

always tended to be on the leading edge of the westward expansion. The names of many Brethren families are indelibly associated with the history of the period. Their offspring played important roles in the growth and the development of numerous states—North Carolina, Kentucky, Ohio, Illinois, Indiana, and others.

The Boone family, claims Mallott, was of mixed Quaker and Brethren origins. If so, the Brethren side (Daniel's mother was allegedly Brethren) seems to have won out (see Mallott, 1954, page 117.) At any rate, this family played a role in the settlement of North Carolina and Kentucky.

The Brethren entered Ohio through two avenues. One of these was the overland way by wagon along trails which are now known as U.S. Route 30 and U.S. Route 40. The other was by means of flatboat down the Ohio River. A strong church was established in southeastern Ohio, rapidly growing from the small beginning laid by John Countryman in Adams County in 1793. Under the leadership of Elder Jacob Miller of Virginia and Elder David Bowman, the Lower Miami church in Montgomery County in western Ohio was organized in 1805. By 1850, a total of fifteen churches had been established in this southern Ohio area. In northeastern Ohio, similar developments were taking place. By 1822, so many Brethren had settled in the Mahoning area that it was deemed feasible to hold Annual Conference there—the first time it had been held west of the Allegheny Mountains.

The opening up of the Ohio River route made it possible for pioneers to enter Kentucky from the north. In 1800, Elder George Wolfe, from Fayette County, Pennsylvania, used this route. He constructed a flatboat about fifteen by fifty feet in size which he used to float his family, horses, wagon, and goods over two hundred fifty miles to western Kentucky.[2] In 1808, two sons of Elder Wolfe moved across the Ohio River and settled in Illinois. There they served as a strong nucleus for a thriving church which was organized in 1812, six years

---

[2]For a description of this adventuresome journey see Virginia Fisher, *The Story of the Brethren* (Brethren Publishing House, 1957), pages 60-68. See also the fictionalized story, *Wilderness Boy*, by Ota Lee Russell (Brethren

before Illinois became a state. George Wolfe, Jr., became widely known over many states as one of the most powerful preachers of the period. Sometimes he was challenged to debate on the doctrines of the church; his logic and his manner of speech and deportment usually gave him the victory.

On one occasion he debated with a Catholic priest in a strong Catholic community over a period of several days. He won so devastatingly that the governor of the territory, who had heard the debate from start to finish, supplied an armed guard of soldiers to accompany him safely away from the area. In Jonesboro, he held a union meeting with a Baptist minister. The services, in which the two men took turns preaching, were largely attended. Finally, the meetings were concluded by a hearty and warm handclasp of goodwill by the two clergymen. The scene made an unforgettable impression on the audience, which included many officials of Union County. An engraver was then employed to make an official county seal which depicted the two clergymen standing with clasped hands (Two Centuries of the Church of the Brethren, 1908, page 395).

Elder Wolfe was also active in behalf of matters of state. In 1818, an effort was made to include in the new constitution a clause approving slavery. Elder Wolfe took a strong stand against slavery and is attributed with doing more than any other one man to prevent Illinois from becoming a slave state.

The church is indebted to him most of all for his missionary activity and his wise supervision among the churches. His leadership was respected and sought in Kentucky, Indiana, and Iowa, as well as in his own state.

In many respects it might be said that during the nineteenth century the growth of the Church of the Brethren paralleled the growth of the country. Its membership was an integral part of the westward migration and the development of new territories. Its ministers, not all of the caliber of Elder Wolfe, were hardworking and faithful. Each local congregation had the tendency to select its most outstanding men as

---

Press, 1956). Another fiction book by the same author tells of the Wolfe era in southern Illinois—*Jackknife Summer*, Brethren Press, 1958.

ministers. As a consequence, each state where the Brethren were well established had a plurality of remarkable leaders whose influence was great not only among the membership of the churches but also among local and state authorities. Any list of the truly superior leaders of the church from 1790 to 1840 would necessarily include many dozen individuals. It is tragic that they are soon forgotten in name and achievement. Today, we too easily take for granted the foundations which they laid and the benefits which are derived from their genius and sacrificial efforts.[3]

Westward migration continued at a rapid pace during the latter half of the nineteenth century. The focus is upon the far West and the role of the railroads. In the vast territories west of the Mississippi River, lands were waiting to be claimed. Few Brethren were attracted by the promise of quick riches from gold discoveries or cattle ranching. Many were attracted, however, by the opportunity to gain good farmlands. The pattern of migration can be correlated with the distribution of suitable farmlands and the establishment of small colonies of the devout in states such as Kansas, Missouri, Iowa, Nebraska, North Dakota, Idaho, California, Oregon, and Washington.

After the publication in 1851 of the *Gospel Visitor* (the ancestor of today's *Messenger*) by Henry Kurtz, a new means of communicating the opportunities of Western settlement was frequently used. Occasionally, news of the far Western congregations were published. Toward the latter part of this period, railroad compaines purchased space in church publications to advertise the attractions and the opportunities of moving to the West. For many years, agents of the railroads

---

[3]A number of sources are available to those who are drawn to the study of the remarkable men and women who were leaders of the church during the last century: Freeman Ankrum, *Sidelights on Brethren History,* the Brethren Press, 1962; John S. Flory, *Builders of the Church,* the Elgin Press, 1925; D. L. Miller and G. B. Royer, *Some Who Led,* Brethren Publishing House, 1912; J. H. Moore, *Some Brethren Pathfinders,* Brethren Publishing House, 1929; *Brethren Builders in Our Century,* Brethren Publishing House, 1952; Inez Goughenour Long, *Faces Among the Faithful,* The Brethren Press, 1962.

"worked" the Brethren communities and attended Annual Conference to promote the development of the areas served by their companies. Mallott (1954, chapters 15 and 16) has described this aspect of the growth of the church, showing how the Brethren before 1900 had not only spanned the continent upon which they were planted in 1719 but had also laid well the foundations for a nationwide denomination. Edward Frantz (*Two Centuries of the Church of the Brethren*, 1908, page 94) reported that in 1891 the membership of the church in the states west of the Mississippi consisted of 10,250 persons, or about one-sixth of the total membership. By 1908, it had increased to 15,570, mostly resulting from migration. Two-thirds of these were located in the five states of Kansas, Iowa, Missouri, North Dakota, and Nebraska. Around two thousand Brethren lived in the three Pacific Coast states in 1908.

The story of the continental diffusion of the Brethren, however, is not a happy one in every respect. There are sad and tragic aspects, too. One result was the isolation and the fragmentation of the church. Congregations became widely separated. Because of lack of strong contact with the Eastern Brethren those in the West sometimes tended to go their own ways doctrinally. Individuals suffered the keen loss of the supporting bonds of family and home congregation back east. Just as close relations and communication can further the common goal of doctrinal and denominational unity, isolation and failure of communication can permit divergence of beliefs and make unity more difficult to maintain. The nineteenth century was a period of denominational schism and splintering. While the doctrinal aspects of this will be taken up in the next chapter, it is appropriate here to call attention to the role which geographic diffusion, isolation, and the consequent decline in communication played in the development of this problem.[4]

Another consequence of migration, sometimes quite serious, was the weakening of some congregations which suffered the brunt of massive population loss. It seemed on rare occasions that an entire colony of Brethren would move leav-

---

[4]For a review of these schisms, see John S. Flory, *Flashlights from History*, Brethren Publishing House, 1932, Part 2, "Disintegration."

ing the home congregation a mere shadow of its former self. Commenting on this result, Edward Frantz (*Two Centuries of the Church of the Brethren,* 1908, pages 95-96), addressing the Bicentennial Conference of the church in 1908, noted that those states receiving immigrants in the West showed marked gain in membership. This was often at the expense of other states which have not been able to make good their losses. He was referring particularly to the states of Missouri, Iowa, Kansas, and Nebraska, where nine out of a total of twelve districts had suffered a decline in membership by the end of the nineteenth century. While other factors undoubtedly entered into these declines, scattered membership, heavy outmigration, and loss of leadership were certainly crucial causes.

Growth and expansion were not limited, of course, to the churches of the West. Missionary activity and strengthening of congregations by means of raising large families were common ingredients of this growth. Large congregations often subdivided and frequently established mission churches to which they gave the assistance of leadership and finances. The missionary activities of Elder John Kline of Virginia, who is reputed to have ridden his horse, Nell, thirty thousand miles in behalf of the Lord's work, are well known.[5] One biographer, Benjamin Funk, claims that Kline was the first Brethren minister to preach aggressively in many West Virginia counties (Funk, 1900, page 244). Kline also went on extended missionary tours in Virginia, Maryland, Ohio, and Indiana and was known widely in the church.

Jacob Leatherman, born in 1787, is less well-known but also remarkable in his own way because of outstanding missionary work in the Middletown Valley of Maryland. He did not like horses but did not allow that to deter him in traveling to preach. Henry (1936, page 242) recalls that Leatherman was called the "walking preacher" and estimates that he walked twenty thousand miles to fill two thousand nine hundred twelve preaching engagements in fifty-six years. Many other outstanding examples could be given to illustrate the

---

[5]For detailed information about John Kline, see Roger E. Sappington, *Courageous Prophet,* The Brethren Press, 1964.

sacrificial effort devoted by faithful ministers and laymen to church extension, which was their first love.

A new factor became important in the growth of the churches east of the Mississippi in the latter half of the century. This was revivalism, the spread of religious fervor by means of mass meetings, a movement which gained rapidly in the nineteenth century. These meetings were held over a period of days or weeks with the aim of converting sinners by means of persuasive preaching. Revivalism spread widely among Protestant denominations and did not leave the Brethren untouched. Its "protracted meetings" were not at first regarded favorably by the conservative Brethren. They believed that membership in the church ought to be sought by applicants only after they had become "settled down" in home and family life and had given careful and thoughtful consideration to the responsibilities of discipleship.

Revivalist preachers were urging baptism upon many individuals who were not well-grounded in the faith. The inducing of emotional contagion was a powerful technique for the conversion of souls. It was indeed a great departure from the old methods of serious and thoughtful Bible study and prayer which had been used by the Pietists and by Mack and his fellow-Brethren in Europe.

Annual Conference took up the question of revivalism in 1858, 1869, and again in 1870. Many opposed the trend. Powerful ministers, meanwhile, were using the revival meeting as an effective method for winning converts even though some new members were neglected and were never fully integrated into the churches.

Among the most famous revivalists of the last century were S. H. Bashor and I. J. Rosenberger. Many other ministers followed effectively and successfully in the revivalist methods. S. H. Bashor is reputed to have been an especially powerful speaker. It is estimated that ten thousand converts were added to the church under his preaching. The yearly revival meeting soon passed into the folkways of the church, to remain until the 1930s and the 1940s, when it seemed to lose its effectiveness.

The late Professor Floyd Mallott, a Brethren historian,

believed that during the revivalist period, roughly from 1850 to 1930 or 1940 in the Church of the Brethren, a subtle transformation took place in the composition of our membership. This was the period in which the church lost not only most of its German ethnicity but also began to assimilate large numbers of people of non-German background. These persons were not well-grounded in the tenets of the faith. Failure to conserve all newly converted members of non-Germanic background resulted in larger numbers of inactive members.

Undoubtedly, factors other than revivalism were operating during this period to modify the German character and the sectarian nature of the church. It should not be assumed—even though sentiment might lead us in this direction—that it would have been best had the church retained intact her German folk culture and kept her sectarian self spotlessly clean from admixture with those who were different. It is only accurate to mention, too, that revivalism was usually practiced in a responsible and practical manner. Many ministers refined the art of evangelistic preaching to an exceedingly high level. The list from James Quinter to Rufus Bucher and John T. Glick would be too long to recall here. The church was richer for the thousands of men, women, and children who were impelled by powerful preaching "to accept Christ as their Savior." Most remained faithful to their conversion experience.

Closely tied to the revivalist movement was the phenomenal interest in religious debating which swept the country in the latter half of the nineteenth century up to the time of World War II. Of course, this was before the time of radio, civic clubs, and television, which now very easily consume our time and interests. During this period, the church was one of the few formal organizations of the community—or the only one. Its services were largely attended by nonmembers as well as by members. Its activities provided a meaningful social function of organizing the interests of the people, breaking the monotony, and legitimizing the moral norms of family and neighborhood life. There was a general interest in religious topics, and people attended religious debates in large numbers. The Brethren were especially active in debating.

These occasions served to augment the fame and the prestige of the German Baptist Brethren, or Dunkers (as they were then popularly known).[6]

The debates would consist of a series of interchanges between clergymen of two denominations, lasting in some instances as long as a week or ten days. The more outstanding ones were recorded by a reporter and then published in full for wider diffusion.

The following debates are among those which have been published; the Brethren representative is named first in each instance. A debate between James Quinter and S. P. Snyder, a Lutheran clergyman, was held in a grove a few miles east of Delphi, Indiana, August 20 to 22, 1867. The attendance was estimated by the moderators at two thousand. The question was "Is immersion the mode of Christian baptism authorized and proved by the Bible?" In 1879, a debate was held in the Lutheran church in Waynesboro, Pennsylvania, between S. H. Bashor and P. Bergstressor. The topics were baptism, the Lord's Supper, and feetwashing. Elder D. F. Stauffer of Beaver Creek, Maryland, was one of the moderators. The debate ran from November 21 until November 27 and was attended by "an immense concourse of people." The debate between J. W. Stein and D. B. Ray in 1880 centered on the issue of whether the Brethren churches could be regarded as true churches of Christ. In Rockingham, Missouri, beginning March 20 and ending March 28, 1889, a debate took place between R. H. Miller and Daniel Sommer of the Church of Christ. Over five hundred pages of transcribed material from this debate have been published. A variety of topics was covered in the debate between B. E. Kesler and H. M. Riggle of the Church of God. The discussions were held September 15 to 26, 1915, in a large Chautauqua tent at North Webster, Indiana. Attendance was estimated to have been twelve hundred people

---

[6]The official name of the church was German Baptist Brethren until its present name was adopted in 1908. However, because of its mode of baptism, it was commonly known as the Dunker Church. The word *Dunker* is an anglicized form derived from the German verb *tunken,* which corresponds to the modern German verb *taufen.*

each night.

One of the results of these debates was to validate the claims of the Brethren to many people. They took on a distinct tone of justification and defense of the Brethren doctrines. The running accounts of the night-to-night discussions were published in numerous daily or weekly newspapers and created interest in religious matters. They were one means by which the Church of the Brethren, through its outstanding spokesmen, came to be more widely known during the period under discussion.

Estimate of Numerical Growth to 1890

After examining some of the factors entering into the growth of the church, it is now desirable to attempt a numerical estimate of this growth. In 1890, the United States government, using figures supplied by Galen B. Royer, reported the Brethren as consisting of 61,101 members, 720 congregations, and 1,622 ministers. Thus, in the space of one hundred years the church had doubled its 1790 membership of 1,515 a total of 5.25 times. If this growth had taken place at a constant rate, the membership would have doubled around every twenty years. The assumption of an even growth at this rate, however, cannot be validated and indeed seems unlikely.

A census of the strength of the Brotherhood was attempted personally by Howard Miller and published privately by him at Lewisburgh, Pennsylvania, in 1882 under the title of *Record of the Faithful*. It was described by the author on the title page as being a statistical record and a complete directory of the Brethren Church for the years 1881-1882. It contained the most thorough information on the church collected up to that time. In addition to listing districts, congregations, and church houses, the ministers were named together with their status in the ministry. By actual membership count, the total strength of the Brotherhood was 57,749—including the Old Order Brethren. Miller admitted being unable to obtain reports from some congregations. Taking this into account, he estimated the total numerical strength of the Brethren at between 55,000 and 60,000, excluding 3,000 members of the Old Order Church who were at that time in the process of separating (page 67).

A great deal of extremely valuable information is contained in Miller's small paperbound booklet. Unfortunately, only a few copies of it remain extant. Therefore, most of the detailed congregational and ministerial information is largely unknown by those who do not have access to this work.

Incidentally, in 1881 the six states containing the largest memberships were: Pennsylvania, 14,557; Indiana, 10,237; Ohio, 9,362; Virginia, 4,965; Illinois, 4,407; and Iowa, 3,056.

In summarizing the period from 1790 to 1890, several observations can be made. First, it was a period of phenomenal numerical growth for the Brethren—a *rate* of growth which we in the second half of the twentieth century have not been able to match. Second, this increase was achieved by means of a variety of methods: home community evangelism, the rearing of large families, the subdividing of congregations, intensive and dedicated missionary activity by many outstanding ministers, extension by means of migration, and finally revivalism. Third, rapid growth and expansion brought about significant changes in the church. The German and sectarian qualities were being inevitably modified as persons of other religious and sociocultural backgrounds were accepted as members. The church was being "Americanized." And finally, geographic spread produced new problems of maintaining denominational cohesion, communication with distant segments, and schism and fragmentation. How these problems were solved, partially through the building up of formal organization and the establishment of publications, will be discussed in another chapter.

The Foreign Mission Movement

The story of the geographic expansion of the Brethren would be incomplete without including the foreign mission activities of the church, for, as a result of this movement, the Church of the Brethren has been planted on five continents—in nine countries besides the United States and Canada.[7] The

---

[7] Brethren congregations have been established in Denmark, Sweden, Turkey, India, China, Nigeria, and Ecuador; missions in France and Switzerland did not develop into congregations.

history of this work has been ably told in the works of Royer and Moyer.[8]

While the modern Protestant foreign missionary movement began with William Carey (1761-1834) of England, its earliest stirrings among the Brethren can be traced back only to around 1852. In that year a query asking whether the Brethren ought not acknowledge the Great Commission to its full extent was considered in the Annual Conference.

In its response to this query, the Conference affirmed the commission in Matthew 28:19-20 to preach the gospel in all the world. No organization or plans, however, were drawn up—and were not to be until nearly thirty years had passed. It may be assumed from this that the Brethren were slow to respond to the challenge of foreign missions. This is perhaps correct. It should be added, however, that many exceedingly difficult changes needed to take place in attitude and organization before the church was willing and able to conduct foreign mission activity.

There was a feeling that there was plenty of evangelistic work to be done here at home. Organizationally and financially, no means were available to conduct missionary work. Brethren had a distrust of unnecessary organization. The giving of money to support ministers was a radical idea. In addition, Brethren had no intimate or clear understanding of the needs beyond their own country—something that D. L. Miller in his travels, lectures, and popular books was to correct before the end of the century.

Despite the inaction of Annual Conference, powerful, highly respected, and well-educated young Brethren were challenged by the needs abroad. Between 1875 and 1900 they were calling the church to "turn to the world." Conservatives objected, but a great idea had taken root in the minds of many. It was a biblical idea and had logical force. It was all but inevitable—given their devotion to obedience to scriptural command—that the Brethren would respond to the call to carry

---

[8]G. B. Royer, *Thirty-three Years of Missions,* Brethren Publishing House, 1913, and Elgin S. Moyer, *Missions in the Church of the Brethren,* Brethren Publishing House, 1931.

their witness to other lands.

The first effort in foreign missions came in 1876 when Christian Hope, an ordained Brethren minister, was sent to his homeland, Denmark, to baptize some persons at their own request. This work was sponsored, significantly, by the Northern Illinois District since the Annual Conference had not yet set up any funds or organization to carry on such activities.

Finally, in 1884 the Conference appointed what was called the "General Church Erection and Missionary Committee," of which D. L. Miller was a member for many years. This group eventually assumed the oversight of the Danish mission, which proved not to be overly successful. The 1950 *Yearbook* of the church was the last to carry a membership listing of the Danish church. Other efforts at mission work took place in Turkey, Sweden, Switzerland, and France with no lasting success. Meanwhile, conviction and enthusiasm were growing. Missions as "the great first-work of the church" were coming to be accepted. During the period of 1890 to 1930, the interest in missions produced a great outpouring of literature and money. Powerful and youthful leaders of the church were effectively doing their work.

The India mission was undertaken in 1894, and the people back home were encouraged with slow but lasting results. The first missionaries in India, arriving in 1895, were Wilbur and Mary Stover and Bertha Ryan. In 1908, Frank and Anna Crumpacker, George Hylton and wife, and Emma Horning arrived in China. Good progress was made there, but repeated political revolution interrupted the program. A high price was paid in sacrifice, hardship, and effort. Those of middle and older age will remember the sorrow and the sense of loss suffered by the entire denomination in the martyrdom in 1937 of Alva and Mary Harsh and Minneva Neher, three of our beloved missionaries in China. Many of our Chinese brethren have also suffered martyrdom, a loss felt less keenly only because few of our stateside members have had a chance to know and love them personally.

Finally, because of political oppression in China, our missionaries were unable to remain. Several families left in 1949 with the remainder staying another year or two. All were gone in 1951, and the young church of around three thousand members planted there has suffered persecution and disbanding.

The Africa field, our most promising one, was opened in 1922 and 1923 when the Albert Helsers, the Stover Kulps, and the Homer Burkes began their work there.

Meanwhile, interest in opening a mission in South America was growing. The gradual withdrawal from China gave additional impetus to the desire to open a new field. Ecuador was chosen, and the first missionaries there were the Benton Rhoades family, going in 1946, and the Claude Wolfes, going in 1948.

The Minutes of Annual Conference for 1980 and 1981 report membership figures for the congregations and local churches in the areas abroad. These members are not reported in Church of the Brethren lists since, in accord with the church's policy of supporting the movement toward independent organization of our mission churches, the members are no longer under Brethren auspices. The number of expatriate missionaries is greatly reduced as a result of the trend to encourage and train clergy and leaders among the nationals.

	Membership	Churches	Missionaries
India	9,500	25	1
Africa	35,000	73	1
Ecuador	300	6	1

These figures reflect only one dimension of the sacrifice, work, and effort which have gone into the growth of the church in other lands. Many victories and many defeats have been sustained in this arm of the church's ministry. Our deepest joy lies in the fact that men, women, and children of other lands have come to share that peace and blessing which come from abiding in the way of Christ.

The mission program of the Church has undergone continual evaluation and modification. New emphases and programs have been launched. These thrusts will be described in Chapter 6.

Growth To The Present Time

During the early part of the Twentieth Century, the rate of church growth continued fairly high. From 1900 to 1940, the membership in the United States increased by a factor of 2.4, from 75,000 to 173,783 in a period of only forty years. From 1940 to 1963, the peak year of church membership, the increase was only 28,474, indicating a very much slower rate of growth. After 1963, Brethren membership declined to a level of 170,839 (1980), a level first reached in the 1930s.

The decline in the growth rate of the denomination since 1940 may be puzzling and difficult to comprehend by the reader. Some attempt, therefore, must be made to examine this trend. A number of factors seems to have produced it. The reader should be cautioned, however, to realize that these factors have not been precisely measured as to their effect on the Church of the Brethren. They stand only as highly probable hypotheses.

The perceptive reader has already noted that the decline in the growth rate began during World War II. It is likely that the war did affect religious phenomena in many ways. It channeled tremendous energies into the economy. A direct consequence of this was a stepped-up rate of mobility and a disruption of the more stable and traditional patterns of community life. People sought high-paying jobs in the cites. Large numbers of men were drafted.

The already-established pattern of rural-urban migration was further increased during the war and has remained very high in the postwar years. The weaker and more marginal rural communities were adversely affected by the mechanization of farming which reduced the number of farmers and farm laborers in the country to less than ten percent of the labor force in 1960. This in itself was a severe blow to the potential growth of our predominantly rural foundations. This has meant that the church is gradually shifting its entire approach, methodology, and sense of values as it seeks to adapt its ministry more to the urban society.

It will be recalled that in past generations a major source of church growth was the large numbers of children reared by our strong rural families. This primary source of church

Growth Data 1890-1982*
The Church of the Brethren

	1890	1906	1916	1926	1936	1946	1956	1966	1976	1980	1981	1982
Membership	61,101	76,547	105,102	128,392	153,516	182,497	195,881	191,549	178,157	170,839	170,267	168,844
Congregations	720	815	997	1,030	1,031**	1,018	1,053	1,058	1,041	1,040	1,045	1,043
Ministers	1,622	1,784	2,984	3,094	3,043	3,286	2,939	2,503	2,342	2,478	1,988	2,310

*These figures do not include overseas membership. In 1980, the total overseas membership was as follows: India, 9,500; Africa, 35,000 and growing rapidly; Ecuador, 300.

**This figure is derived from the Yearbook for 1946.

membership growth has been greatly reduced. The birthrate of the country as a whole reached an all-time low in the worst years of the depression. It rebounded somewhat during the 1950s but has resumed its decline in the 1960s. In 1968 it had fallen to the low of the depression years. This means that our denomination can count on only a minimal growth through natural increase—and that only if the congregations are able to conserve most or all of their youth for the church.

Over the past thirty years, marked changes have taken place in the social organization of community life. One of these changes has been the phenomenal increase of clubs and formal groups which compete with the church for allegiance and membership. This is a far cry from the nineteenth century, when churches were often the centers of community life and had little if any competition from other formal organizations. At that time, it was not uncommon for large numbers of nonmembers to attend religious services because few if any other forms of organized community life existed. No longer can we take for granted that people will be interested in the church simply because few other organizations exist to attract them. Today the church shares the community scene with a large number of competing groups and interests.

The decline of the revivalist movement among the Brethren has already been mentioned. Many congregations today have entirely given up the custom of holding evangelistic meetings. They no longer seem successful generally in reaching the unchurched of the community. Church membership classes are being substituted as an effective means for preparing the youth of our own families for baptism.

There is also the possibility that churches were paring their membership rolls more severely as support of district and denominational programs came more and more to be put on a per capita basis. It did not seem sensible to local churches to have outreach allocations based upon membership lists containing large numbers of people who had become inactive or who had moved away to some other community.

Finally, less tangible changes in the relative emphasis of values and doctrines in the church must be mentioned. These changes are more difficult to measure, and awareness of them is more intuitively based. The more traditional values placed upon "saving souls," going to heaven, and avoiding hell are not as urgently held today—either by the Christian or by the non-Christian. As our denomination moves from its more sectarian background toward a more churchlike form, local evangelism tends to be left to the care of the salaried pastor and perhaps to irregularly active lay groups which may or may not be very successful. Church membership itself is not regarded as the most crucial issue. Stress is placed, rather, upon an effectively run church program and more recently upon involvement and dialogue with the secular order. Now the crucial issue tends to be seen as the personal and social relevancy of the church and its active participation in the arena of community and national problems.

The decline in church membership since 1963 has been a great concern to the churches. In 1979, a thoroughgoing study by an Annual Conference committee was begun. This committee's report was adopted by the 1981 Annual Conference. It contained a careful analysis of the reasons for the decline in church membership and offered many concrete suggestions designed to alleviate the problem of membership decline. One of the goals of the 1980s is to enlarge the mission of the church to more effectively bring the reconciling knowledge of Christ to increased numbers of people. We will examine this calling again in Chapter 6.

4

Brethren Beliefs

Introduction

The origin and the development of Brethren beliefs is an intriguing area of study. Our major concern in this chapter will be to describe the beliefs of the church founders and trace their development in a general way up to the present time. So that the reader may go more deeply into the study, the more important resources upon which the author relied will be indicated. This chapter does not presume to represent a definitive statement of doctrine or to represent original research. Its purpose is considerably less pretentious—to inform the reader of the probable source of our doctrines in a general way and to assess the forces that have brought change. For the purposes of this study the world *doctrine* refers to a belief or principle which has authoritative or widespread acceptance in the church. It may relate to a purely abstract entity such as an idea about the nature of the Godhead. On the other hand, it may refer to the beliefs which support or defend sacraments, ceremonies, or ordinances.

It is often asserted that the average person does not have a good understanding of the doctrines of his church. Without remarking upon the validity of this assertion, it is certainly appropriate to hope that the level of doctrinal knowledge can be increased. The present chapter is dedicated to this aim.

A high degree of importance should be given to the materials about to be discussed. The Church of the Brethren has never put forth an official statement of doctrine, claiming instead the entire New Testament as its creed. It is admittedly easier to have good familiarity with a creed which may be used frequently in a worship service than to have equal knowledge of the New Testament as a whole. Therefore, the study of doctrine is especially needed and all members of the denomination should be encouraged to engage in it.

Doctrinal Backgrounds and Sources

It may have occurred already to the reader that the original eight Brethren in 1708 did not suddenly come forth with a totally new set of beliefs which were unique and new in the world. Doctrinally, as well as in other ways, these first Brethren were the recipients of a rich cultural heritage going back many hundreds of years. An attempt to write about those religious principles which were accepted by the Brethren must therefore include a discussion of the major groups and their belief systems with which Mack and his associates were in close contact. This contact may have been direct and personal with the leaders of movements. Other values may simply have been passed down in the religious culture from previous generations. Some aspects such as patterning or emphasis are new and distinctive and arise out of the unique situation to which the Brethren responded.

An adequate discussion of our doctrines—either contemporary or historical—would need to include those which we share with other Christians as well as those which we uniquely possess or emphasize. Quite frequently, however, discussions tend to stress the unique at the expense of losing sight of the common Christian heritage which we share with other Christian bodies. Such discussions fail to maintain a *good balance* of doctrinal emphasis. The tendency for a religious group in Western culture to stress its distinctive attributes is due to the need for its membership to justify and defend its existence and individuality.

The general approach to our topic is diagrammatically represented in Figure 1, which is entitled the Circle of Christian Doctrine, expressing the unity and the distinctiveness of Christendom in 1708. It will be noted that the outer ring implies the existence of a body of prized and basic beliefs which are possessed by all Christians, Protestants and Catholics

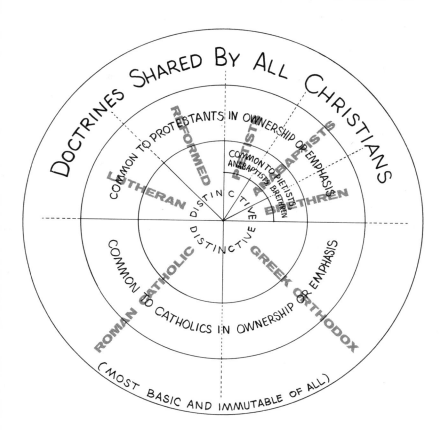

Figure 1. The Circle of Christian Doctrine

alike. These relate to the commonly held beliefs which center in God, Christ, the Holy Spirit, man, the Bible, the church, sin, salvation, and so on. The second or inner ring which is dissected implied the existence of doctrines which are held by either Protestants or Catholics, but not by both. On the Protestant side, these would relate to the doctrinal emphases which produced and/or characterized the Reformation and which are common to Lutheran, Reformed, Pietist, Anabaptist, and Brethren. On the Catholic side of the second ring would be included doctrines relating to matters which Protestants would not accept: the authority of Rome and the pope, the priesthood, the Virgin Mary, St. Peter, and many others. The third circle, or quarter circle, denotes the existence of a common body of beliefs and emphases which is shared by Pietists and Anabaptists. The Brethren share them also because they have gained these doctrines from both the Pietists and the Anabaptists. At the same time, of course, all three of these groups share in major Protestant doctrines and also in doctrines prized by all Christians represented by the outer circle. At the center, certain distinctive beliefs or emphases are implied. There are very few doctrines which are completely unique to any single group. The way they *are emphasized*, however, may be quite distinctive in many respects. It is likely in the patterning and organization of doctrines that the highest degree of uniqueness among most Protestant denominations lies.

The Protestant Character of Brethren Belief

The first eight members of our church were reared within the cultural environment of German Protestant Christianity. Seven of the eight were devout Reformed Christians. The other was a Lutheran. In organizing a separate Christian body, they were not rejecting the basic doctrines of the Christian faith. They would have affirmed, with some few exceptions, the catalogue of doctrines of either the Lutheran or the Reformed Church.[1]

In 1717, six Brethren from the Solingen area were imprisoned for the "crime" of being baptized. During their four-year imprisonment they were questioned repeatedly concerning their beliefs. The record of these examinations serves as a reliable source of information concerning Brethren doctrines. The Solingen Brethren repeatedly affirmed the Heidelberg

---

[1]It has been noted that most of the early Brethren were from the Reformed Church and that they remained in basic doctrinal agreement with the Protestant heritage which this represented. The author knows of no thorough study of the extent or the nature of Brethren indebtedness to the Reformed Church. Most studies have focused upon our indebtedness to the Pietists and the Anabaptists. Perhaps this line of doctrinal studies can be emphasized in the future.

Catechism of the Reformed Church and stated to the examining committee, " . . . if only the infant baptism, swearing of oaths, and the sixtieth question [on justification by faith] were different, we could then soon agree with you" (Durnbaugh, 1958, pages 249-250). This statement well illustrates the common doctrinal grounds upon which the Brethren stood with Protestant Christians of the period. William Willoughby, who has made a thorough and scholarly study of the beliefs of the Brethren in Europe, has noted their kinship with and indebtedness to Protestant Christianity and to the Reformation. He states that the Brethren "believed, first of all, in the basic doctrines of the Christian faith as defined by the historic creeds" (Willoughby, 1951, pages 150-151).

That the Brethren still perceived themselves two hundred years later to be consistent in their doctrine with Protestant Christianity in general is well illustrated in a statement made by H. C. Early, a much-beloved and highly respected minister of the church. Elder Early delivered an address before the Annual Conference in 1908 on the subject of the doctrines of the Brethren. Before discoursing upon the distinctive beliefs of the church, he stated, "First, let it be understood that the Protestant Churches, for the most part, agree on the large and fundamental doctrines of the New Testament" (*Two Centuries of the Church of the Brethren*, page 133). He then set forth fifteen or eighteen doctrines upon which the Brethren are united with other Protestant bodies.

Space will not permit a study of the basic doctrines of the Christian Church. The reader may be referred to the work of several Brethren scholars for more extensive treatment of these matters.[2] D. W. Kurtz, for example, treats among others, the doctrines of God, man, sin, Christ, salvation, the church, the Holy Spirit, faith, Christian experience, future things, and the Scriptures. It is important to stress that to be Brethren does not mean only to be distinctive or unique. To be Brethren

---

[2]D. W. Kurtz, *et al., Studies in Doctrine and Devotion*, Brethren Publishing House, Eighth Printing, 1946; and William M. Beahm, *Studies in Christian Belief*, Brethren Press, 1958.

means to be Christian and to be Protestant as well. On these principles the founders of the church were in accord. To them they gave unswerving conviction and devotion. They recognized their theological kinship with Luther and Calvin and the rest of the leaders of the Protestant Reformation.

The Influence of the Anabaptist Beliefs

Mack and the early Brethren had ample opportunity for continuous and extensive familiarity and contact with the Anabaptists (sometimes called *Taufgesinnte*). In 1708, several hundred families of them were living in the Palatinate, many of them having moved there from Switzerland. That Mack visited in the congregations of the Anabaptists (Mennonites) is clearly mentioned by his son, Alexander Mack, Jr., in the preface to the 1774 edition of his father's book (Durnbaugh, 1958, pages 120-121). From this we may infer that where Brethren and Mennonite beliefs overlap there is a strong likelihood of Brethren indebtedness to the older group for those beliefs. Of course, the Pietists shared some of the Anabaptist ideas, and Mack was also greatly influenced by them.

Anabaptist Beliefs

It now remains for us to examine the beliefs of the Anabaptists and to compare them with those of the Brethren. The following list is useful for this purpose.[3]
1. Adult baptism and the invalidity of infant baptism.
2. Individual responsibility to God; free will (free choice) on the part of each person.
3. The true church as being the elect or the regenerate.
4. Imitation of primitive Christianity; the apostolic church.

---

[3]I am indebted to Dr. William Willoughby (1951) for his excellent discussion of the Anabaptist beliefs and their relation to the Brethren. Also helpful are two articles by Durnbaugh (1959) entitled "The Genius of the Early Brethren." On the Anabaptists, the reader may consult H.S. Bender, "The Anabaptist Vision," in *The Recovery of the Anabaptist Vision* (Scottdale: Herald Press, 1957) or F. H. Littell, *The Anabaptist View of the Church,* 2nd edition (Boston: Starr King, 1958).

5. Acceptance of the Scriptures, especially the New Testament, as the final authority in religious matters; the right of individual interpretation of the Scriptures under the guidance of the Holy Spirit.
6. Acceptance of the God-given authority of the government in civic matters; denial of the right of the secular government to intrude in spiritual matters. No force in religion. A Christian not permitted to hold civil office for fear of compromising his behavior, especially in being connected with capital punishment and warfare.
7. Affirmation rather than an oath.
8. Refusal to bear arms or to do military service.
9. Salvation and an inner spiritual experience of God on the part of the sincere believer.
10. Baptism not a sacrament, but a rite accepted in faith and marking entrance into the church.
11. The Lord's Supper not a sacrament but a commemorative rite to be participated in by the elect only.
12. Washing of the feet of the saints as a mark of obedience and humility.
13. Consistency between faith and works rather than justification by faith alone.
14. The necessity of the ban or excommunication for unfaithfulness together with avoidance of all social contacts (shunning) of members placed under the ban.

After analyzing the beliefs of the Anabaptists or Mennonites and observing the contact that Mack had with them, Willoughby comments that there is "no item in this list to which the early Brethren could not have agreed. . . . It is enough here to note that the structure of Anabaptist credenda is very similar to the system of beliefs held by the early Brethren" (Willoughby, 1951, pages 71-72).

Mack himself stresses the doctrinal similarity of the Brethren with the old Anabaptists in his little book, *Basic Questions*, Question 33. He concludes his answer to his son's question concerning the doctrines of the Anabaptists by saying, "We are completely agreed with them as far as their doctrine is concerned, which does not teach anything in contradiction to the gospel" (Durnbaugh, 1958, page 340).

Although this statement has a high probability of being valid, it would be unwarranted for the reader to assume that there were no differences between the doctrines or the practices of the Mennonites and those of the Brethren of this period. Furthermore, those differences were regarded as important ones. The differences which marked the Mennonites and the Brethren concerned minor aspects of the principles stated above. Baptism is a good example of this. The two bodies agreed as to the nature and the importance of baptism but differed as to its method of application, with the Brethren holding to trine immersion in a forward manner and the Mennonites permitting pouring. There were other disagreements of a similar order relating to the Anabaptist tenets.

Even more important, the Brethren were distinguished from the German Anabaptists of the period in that they held *additional principles* not subscribed to by the latter. Some of these the Schwarzenau Brethren got from the Pietists. Others had to do with the emphasis or importance placed on the various beliefs. Some differences were social, having to do with the exceedingly unsavory but undeserved image which had grown up around the Anabaptists over the one hundred fifty years of their existence in Germany. Mack also regarded many Anabaptists of his day as unregenerate.

The Influence of Pietist Beliefs

Mack and his associates had extensive familiarity and contacts with Pietists. The founder had read the works of Felbinger, Arnold, Hochmann, and perhaps others. That these contacts had important influence on the Schwarzenau Brethren is testified by numerous church historians who have examined the matter.

Donald Miller made a careful study of the writings of Gottfried Arnold in an attempt to assess their influence on Mack. He concludes that the writings of the famous Pietist "had a major influence upon the lives of the Early Brethren" (Miller, 1960, page 39).

John L. Gillin wrote his Ph.D. dissertation on the topic of the Dunkers. Noting the extensive relations of Mack with the

Pietist Hochmann as they traveled on preaching tours together, he states, "From a comparison of the teachings of these two men it is easy to draw the conclusion that Mack was an apt disciple" (Gillin, 1906, page 36).

The well-known Brethren historian and former governor of Pennsylvania, M. G. Brumbaugh, was so impressed with the Pietist influence of Hochmann's confession of faith on the Brethren that he reprinted it in two places in his book, *A History of the Brethren.* He decided that Mack had "used it as the basis of his rites and ordinances of the congregation" (Brumbaugh, 1899, page 83). Perhaps Brumbaugh has overstressed Mack's indebtedness to Hochmann. There were elements of Hochmann's Pietism which Mack rejected.

Of the influence of Hochmann, Durnbaugh writes that it was he "who 'awakened' most of those people who became the early brethren. . . . [t]hey originally looked to him as their spiritual guide" (1958, page 36).

Since Pietism was mediated to the early Brethren in significant part through Hochmann, it is appropriate to summarize the major points of his confession (see Brumbaugh, 1899, pages 83-88).

1. He accepts and is in accord with the major doctrines of orthodox Christianity.
2. He accepts only adult baptism.
3. He holds that the Lord's Supper is to be celebrated only by the elect who have renounced the sinful life.
4. He accepts Christian perfection but claims not to have achieved it.
5. He believes that Christ alone is the head of the church, though ministers may be qualified for office by the Holy Spirit.
6. He holds that government is by divine right in civil matters but its power does not extend to spiritual matters.
7. He states his belief in the "final restoration of damned men."

Though he did not include it in the confession, Hochmann believed also that (1) organized churches were as Babylon and that organization was neither necessary nor in accord with primitive Christianity (this is the point at which Mack separated from Hochmann); (2) marriage was a less holy state than celibacy. He described a total of five different kinds of marriage. Gillin (1906, page 39) attributes these beliefs to the influence of Arnold's book, *A True Portraiture of Primitive Christianity*. He thought that Mack was also familiar with Arnold's book and probably was influenced by it at first to regard marriage, while ordained by God, as nevertheless lower than the celibate state and perhaps to experiment in Schwarzenau with communal holding of property as described in the book of Acts. Of the above summary of Hochmann's beliefs, it is probably correct to say that the Schwarzenau Brethren would have accepted them all, except, of course, the belief that the elect of God ought not to organize into a church.

The writings of Gottfried Arnold can be taken also as representative of Pietism. Miller's study (1960, pages 39-50) is helpful here. The following elements are stressed by Arnold.

1. The necessity for repentance which involves turning away from the world, self-denial, and *absolute obedience* to Christ and the New Testament.

2. Continued search for subsequent enlightenment and awakening through prayer, Bible study, the devotional life, and fasting. As a result of this quest for illumination, an inner experience of sweetness and confidence is reached.

3. Pious behavior and presentation of sincere godly life without hypocrisy to all people as a witness of Christ's redeeming love. Miller, 1960, regards this as possibly one of the most distinctive emphases of the Brethren among Protestants.

4. The wrongness of elaborate, expensive, and prideful churches and cathedrals. Looking back to the primitive church, which met in simple houses, he emphasized that the genuine place of worship is the human heart.

5. Condemnation of the elevation of the clergy and of the distinction between clergy and laity. Teachers or spokesmen were to be selected by the congregation to serve as coworkers in their midst.

6. The degeneration of Christianity under the Emperor Constantine (324 A.D.), who made it the state religion of Rome. The organized churches continue in this fallen state. The true church consists of the "awakened" who are called out from the existing churches to become the elect or regenerate.

7. The composition of creeds as a means by which the clergy of the fallen churches could exert conformity and authority over the people and punish heretics. Therefore, his attitude was one of distrust of creeds.

In respect to the matter of creeds, it is significant to note that Mack and the early Brethren opposed the adopting of a creed. This was presumably because it might hinder continued enlightenment and fix in an unchanging form the doctrines and beliefs of the church. It seems clear that the Christian life was regarded as a process of continued development and growth on the part of both the church as a body of believers and the individual seeker after truth.

While there is little in the above statements of Pietist beliefs to which the Brethren could not agree, Durnbaugh (1959), discussing "The Genius of the Brethren," reminds us that several aspects of radical Pietism were discarded by the Brethren founders. These rejected ideas are: the concept of a purely spiritual church having no organization or outward forms; extreme individualism in interpreting the Scriptures; strong emphasis upon celibacy and devaluation of marriage; extreme mysticism; and community of goods. In spite of some reports[4] that the Schwarzenau Brethren practiced celibacy and the community of goods and desisted from labor for a few years after 1708, there is no hard evidence to support it. Durnbaugh presents evidence to show that at Schwarzenau the Brethren held property as private owners. It is more accurate to state simply that for a few years the Brethren had notable differences of opinion regarding these aspects of Pietism. In a short time Mach could write of these ideas that they were "imbibed er-

---

[4]The *Ephrata Chronicle*, page 2, and Mack in his booklet on fundamental questions (question and answer 37) both report the involvement of the early Brethren with these Pietistic beliefs.

rors" and imply that there was contention among the Brethren until these particular Pietistic doctrines were given up.

With respect to celibacy, there is no evidence that it was ever made a rule or regarded as a requirement of the church. While Mack's book reveals his acceptance of celibacy as a higher state than marriage, marriage itself was not devalued. It was accepted as God-given and as a holy state (Bittinger, 1951, pages 12-15). Mack himself was married and several of his children were born after the founding of the church. On the other hand, given the high value placed upon celibacy, it is quite possible that both at Schwarzenau and at Krefeld individuals may have sought to conform to the norm of sexual abstinence. The *Chronicle* refers to the presence of a number of unmarried Brethren at Krefeld. It seems quite certain, however, that no emphasis was placed upon this teaching after the Brethren emigrated to Pennsylvania. It was one of the Pietist doctrines which receded of its own weight.

In summary, a study of the beliefs of the Pietists reveals them to be consistent with the authoritative teachings of the early Brethren, excluding of course the exceptions noted above. In actuality, the Schwarzenau group was Pietist in its origin. Mack was indebted to Hochmann, Arnold, and other Pietists for a strong influence on the ideas he held. Excepting as qualified, the central doctrines of Anabaptism and Pietism are indicative of Brethren belief. They can be taken as Brethren *so far as they go*. Mack and the others were in agreement with them, and therefore they became established in the body of Brethren belief.

And yet, Mack and his group were not satisfied with Pietist and Anabaptist beliefs alone. They decided to adventure further in their Christian experience. And now there remains the task of discovering the aspects of Brethren belief and practice which are distinctive.

Distinctive Brethren Doctrines and Emphases

The church is fortunate, from the historical standpoint, in the fact that Alexander Mack, while still in Germany, published two works which set forth the beliefs of the early Brethren. These are entitled *Basic Questions*, probably first published in 1713, and *Rights and Ordinances,* first published in 1715.[5] More recent editions of these works contain valuable historical materials in the preface written by Alexander Mack, Jr.

Undoubtedly, the most outstanding theme of Mack's writting is his stress on obedience to the scriptural commandments and his desire to conform to the order of the New Testament church. It is this same conviction which did not permit him either to align himself with the Mennonites or to remain with Hochmann and the Pietists.

Mack and the others by taking up with Hochmann and the Pietists had gradually become convinced that their own infant baptism in the state churches was invalid and contrary to the commands of the Scriptures. This left them in an unbaptized state. Had they been willing, they might have cast their destiny with the Mennonites, who would have rebaptized them. Mack could not take this course because he believed that the Mennonites were degenerate because of their not being fully obedient to the scriptural commands as he accepted them.

Some of the Pietists had resolved this problem by staying in the state churches where they could act as a leaven and continue to regard their baptism as valid. The radical or separatistic Pietists resolved the issue by denying the need for membership in an organized church and by claiming the validity of a baptism by the Holy Spirit. They believed that God accepted a spiritual renewal and an inward conformity and that an outward conformity through water baptism is not to be made a necessary requirement for salvation. Hochmann comments on the Schwarzenau baptism in the Eder in a letter written on November 2, 1708, by saying, "Whether to baptize or not to baptize must be left free" (Durnbaugh, 1958, page 126).

Mack was not so easily satisfied. His extensive study of early church history and of the Scriptures together with his unconditional acceptance of scriptural authority led him to the

---

[5]These two books have been published in many different editions, usually under the titles *Ground-Searching Questions* and *Rites and Ordinances.* The most recent and easily available discussion of them is found in Durnbaugh, 1958, pages 321-324. Durnbaugh has also retranslated both works and included them in his book, thus making them widely available to the interested reader.

conviction that baptism was required as an outward work of obedience resulting necessarily from genuine faith in God. Consequently, during the spring and the summer of 1708, Mack, his wife, and six others entered into prolonged Bible study and prayer to decide their course of action. Out of this experience came the conviction that if they were to be fully obedient to Christ, they must be baptized. Their studies also convinced them that as a body of baptized, regenerate Christians they must be fully obedient to all other scriptural commands relating to how they conducted themselves both in matters of the heart and in "outward" practices and ordinances. The first eight explain their decision and actions in a letter prepared in the summer of 1708 and distributed among the Palatine Pietists (Durnbaugh, 1958, pages 115-120). It is a valuable document that permits us to understand more fully the reasoning of our church founders. This, together with the Mack writings, provide us with the best original sources concerning Brethren thought at the time.

The study of histories of the early church and of the scriptural references to baptism led Mack to the conclusion that baptism should be practiced as a threefold forward immersion in the name of the Father, the Son, and the Holy Spirit. In establishing this pattern, Mack did not maintain that it was the baptism itself which brought salvation. This was the work of the Holy Spirit within the vital inner experience of the soul. Baptism, communion, the Lord's Supper, and so on were not sacraments or magical rites effective in themselves. They were a true and scriptural test of faith—a sign that the redeemed person was willing to accept obedience and submission unto Christ. It was not maintained that water baptism in a threefold forward manner constituted the saving ritual. Salvation was the result of the inner submission to and the presence of Christ.

In his letter to Mack and Grebe, Hochmann besought the Schwarzenau Brethren not to make outward water baptism a requirement or to "exclude from love others who do not look on this as you do" (Durnbaugh, 1958, page 114). History reveals, however, that the Brethren made full obedience to the commands of the Scriptures (as interpreted by them) a sign of the spiritual regeneracy of the individual. They took the willingness to submit to God and his Word *to represent* thepresence of salvation as a true inner experience. In other words, an unwillingness to submit to the ordinances was taken to represent an *invalid* inner experience. It was assumed that enlightenment and Christ's presence had not yet been attained.

The same approach was taken with respect to the Lord's Supper, feetwashing, and the Ten Commandments. This included a literal obedience to the command not to kill, which was extended to forbid participation in war and capital punishment. The doctrines of the simple life, self-denial, nonresistance, nonswearing, the holy kiss, anointing for healing, excommunication, and avoidance (shunning) were built up and elaborated according to the principle of obedience.

If there is any single general principle which marks the Brethren as distinctive and explains their origin, it is their devotion to a full and complete obedience to Christ as revealed in the New Testament. This principle was not only applied to the pious and godly life; it found its expression also in the patterning of the ordinances and the doctrines of the church. Against the background of the preceding discussion, it is now possible to examine those doctrines and practices which became established among the early Brethren and which received strong emphasis. The statement which follows is not to be taken as either an official statement of the church or as a complete listing of the church beliefs.

Brethren Doctrines of the Early Eighteenth Century

1. *Church life, beliefs, ordinances.* The determining principles are the authority of the Bible, the teachings of Christ, and the pattern of the New Testament church as described by the Scriptures and church history.

Involved are the communion of the bread and the cup; the Lord's Supper; washing of the feet at the Lord's Supper; the holy kiss; the laying on of hands; anointing of the sick; appropriate attire in worship; kneeling in prayer; adult baptism by trine immersion in a forward position; the lay ministry; reconciliation of disputes by Matthew 18; zeal and fervor in witness, prayer, and preaching; marriage within the church membership; no formal or official creed but an openness to new truth; plainness and simplicity in worship and church organization; the home as a meeting place for worship; final restoration; the true church consisting of only the fully obedient children of God; firm church discipline including the ban and avoidance (shunning).

2. *The personal life of the individual.* The determining principle is strict obedience to the Scriptures according to the Brethren understanding of them as pertaining to godly and exemplary living.

This principle expressed itself in: prayerful manner; love of the brethren; mercy; humility; honesty; hospitality; brotherliness, nonviolence or nonresistance; temperance, modesty; plainness and simplicity of life, dress and home furnishing; cleanness of language; sexual purity; nonconformity to the world; nonoath taking.

3. *Relation to the state.* The Brethren were law-abiding and submissive to the state in all matters wherein they deemed the state had God-given authority. They denied that the state had a right to intrude in matters of spiritual life.

They believed in: separation of church and state; no force in religion; no recourse to lawsuits to settle disputes; resistance to the draft and refusal to bear arms; no holding of civil office. They believed that to become involved with the state was to become unequally yoked with nonbelievers and to be subjected to the temptation to compromise. In matters where God's command conflicted with the command of the state (*e.g.*, bearing arms, taking oaths), they were obedient first to God and refused to submit to the state.

4. *Relation to other Christians.* The Brethren accepted the view that the true church consisted of God's elect called out to be separate from the world. The elect consisted of those who were fully obedient to the Scriptures and who had been awakened or enlightened through the study of the Scriptures and the guidance of the Holy Spirit. In their early history, the Brethren tended to regard themselves as the elect and other Christians as unregenerate. The salvation of the unregenerate was to be gained by their full obedience to the teachings of the

Bible as the Brethren taught them or by God's mercy in the final restoration.

The Developing Character of Brethren Belief and Thought

The first several decades following 1708 may be thought of as a period of doctrinal establishment and stabilization. Some religious practices were begun and then abandoned. Others were in the process of being further worked out or finding an appropriate emphasis. This was not necessarily a rational procedure, for trial and error and practical considerations were important. One should avoid assuming that Brethren thought and belief were fully established in 1708 and remained unchanged from then on. In actuality, change and development set in immediately.

The fluidity of the Brethren in doctrine and practice, instead of being regarded as undesirable, may be seen as being quite consistent with certain basic presuppositions which they held. Miller, in discussing the influence of Gottfried Arnold, has pointed out the attitude which he took toward the church creeds. He regarded them as instruments of coercion which could readily be brought to bear on the faithful as well as the heretic as a means of gaining conformity. Mack and his group had already noted the imperviousness of the creeds to the new light which Arnold's work on primitive Christianity had revealed. In addition, a basic tenet of Pietism was the search for continued enlightenment and illumination toward an increasingly pious thought and life.

Consequently, the Brethren were distrustful of creeds. They desired not to fix their current beliefs and publish them as a finished work. They believed that they might obtain further knowledge and truth concerning the Scriptures. It would be difficult to change a creed. It could too easily be used to prevent the intrusion of greater insight and the removal of past errors.[6]

---

[6]The rationale of the German sectarians concerning the undesirability of adopting a creed is well expressed in a conversation between Michael Wohlfahrt and Benjamin Franklin which may be found printed in Brumbaugh (1899, page 527).

Following the first baptism in 1708, the Brethren continued to discuss and to study the Scriptures seeking new understanding of their teachings. Radical doctrines which had arisen among the Pietists—such as separatism, mysticism, individualism in spiritual experience, community of goods, and celibacy—were carefully considered and rejected. It is not difficult to comprehend why such beliefs would receive consideration by dissatisfied religious people in Germany at this time. Religious fervor and turmoil were deeply embedded in the life and the culture of the people of this period. Salvation was a primary aim of life. The orthodox churches were far from God in life and practice. Radical solutions were called for. The Brethren were traveling an uncharted course, in all sincerity following the best insights they had.

Credit must be given to the early Brethren for their willingness to modify their position and to give up inappropriate doctrinal emphases. This has been one aspect of the genius of the Brethren in their two hundred seventy-five years of history. They have developed with the movement of history. As we note these changes across time, we shall see that some of them were not always regarded as desirable. Some were resisted in vain. Others brough division and anguish. Very frequently, the impetus for change was not well understood. The kinds of changes that we will note were most frequently a response to conditions and circumstances present at the time. These adjustments of beliefs and practices served the vital role of keeping the church and its emphases in touch with the times—that is, more relevant. This characteristic belongs to the church throughout its history. Perhaps in our own day, more than at any other time, the responsiveness of the church's doctrines and emphases to human need is most critical. The church is in creative tension with society and culture. This is the key not only to its survival but to its vitality.

The Ephrata Movement

In Ephrata, Pennsylvania, stand the remaining buildings—now a historical park—of a religious society which brought considerable pain and self-examination to the

Brethren between 1725 and 1768. Conrad Beissel, a convert baptized by Peter Becker, began to teach radical doctrines and to build up a following. He was a powerful preacher, a disciplined ascetic, and a driving taskmaster. Not all of those attracted to him were able to endure, but many did. From these he welded together a prosperous and self-supporting monastic community which came to be known as the Ephrata Cloisters.

Around 1745, Beissel and his associates established a printing press which sent a flood of devotional and religious materials into the homes of the German-speaking people throughout the colonies. A productive farm and an orchard were begun. As the community prospered, a grist mill, a saw mill, a flax seed oil mill, a fulling mill, a paper mill, and a bark mill were added. Also, a tannery was set up. The sisters operated looms and made cloth. The economic and religious impact on the surrounding area was considerable.

Among other principles, Beissel taught the superiority of celibacy over marriage, communal property, mysticism, and the seventh day as the true Sabbath. He was tireless in proselyting. Among his converts were many Brethren, including Alexander Mack, Jr., and a number of other persons from the Germantown church. Beissel's power lay in his personality and in his ability to appeal to the Pietistic leanings of the Brethren. Also, he met them on their own ground of obedience to the Word.

That Beissel had many converts from the Brethren is not surprising. The entering into and the leaving of Brethren from the Ephrata Cloisters lasted for several decades. And yet, the measurable impact of Ephrata upon Brethren doctrine was in the end minimal. One reason was that the monastic community was continually shaken with disharmony and conflict. The asceticism was severe and the regimen harsh. While continence was not mandatory of all monastics, the married were deemed to be spiritually inferior. Not all could endure the Beissel administration. Many Brethren returned to their congregations; among them was Alexander Mack, Jr.

In some respects the Ephrata movement may be regarded as a temptation to revert to some of the radical doctrines of Pietism which they had given up in Europe. Mysticism, celibacy, sexual abstinence, community of goods, and separatism as symbolized in the fascinating and yet controversial personality of Conrad Beissel were strangely attractive to many of the Pennsylvania sectarians.

That the church weathered the crisis posed by Beissel's efforts is probably due to the radical quality of the movement together with the growing solidarity and a sense of community which were developing among the prospering Brethren congregations. And yet, included in the complex history of interrelationships between those at Ephrata and the Brethren over nearly fifty years is a vast amount of tragedy, frustration, and sorrow. The story has been told repeatedly by secular and church historians alike. It constitutes a fascinating chapter of Brethren development.

Brethren Convictions Tested
During the Revolutionary War

No great crisis in Brethren thought emerged until the period of the Revolutionary War when conditions became exceedingly severe in Pennsylvania. During the period from 1776 to 1780, their faithfulness to the doctrine of nonviolence was put to a severe test.[7] The Brethren suffered defamation, loss of property, and physical violence because of their refusal to bear arms or to take sides against the British. Laws were passed requiring the Brethren to take an oath of allegiance to the state and to pay money in lieu of military service. The latter they could do but not the former. Since they had refused the oath of allegiance, their political status was ambiguous in the eyes of radicals and riffraff who sometimes took opportunity to rob, beat, and torment the Brethren pacifists.

The story of Christopher Sauer, Jr., is worthy of special attention. Sauer's father, of Germantown, had built up a pros-

---

[7]For the most thorough study of the problems of the Brethren during the colonial period and the Revolutionary War, see R. D. Bowman, *The Church of the Brethren and War* (Brethren Publishing House, 1944), Chapter III. The account of Christopher Sauer, Jr., and his persecution is given there. See also Donald F. Durnbaugh, ed., *The Brethren in Colonial America* (The Brethren Press, 1974) and Steve Longenecker, *The Christopher Sauers* (The Brethren Press, 1981).

perous printing establishment, specializing in publishing papers, almanacs, and books for the German sectarians. The two Sauers, father and son, were perhaps the most influential Germans in the colonies. Both were godly men. Sauer, Jr., a Brethren, refused to swear allegiance to the state. The Revolutionary government decided to make an example of him by humiliating him publicly and by confiscating his property. The latter was done illegally. Sauer, Jr., died in poverty but he remained faithful to the end.

The Sauer press had been a major unifying and educational influence upon the Brethren. With its demise, the church suffered a major loss. With the change of government brought about by the war and the increase of unfavorable sentiment toward the German sectarians, many became convinced that by migrating to the South and the West their situation would be improved. With the increasing tendency of the Brethren to migrate to more distant areas, new doctrinal problems presented themselves.

Maintaining Doctrinal Unity in The Post-Revolutionary Period

Preserving doctrinal conformity was seldom a grave problem within the closely knit and more populous Brethren communities of Pennsylvania and Maryland. Strong social and cultural influences effectively preserved the religious patterns there. It was a different matter with the smaller, more distant communities in North Carolina, Kentucky, and Illinois. There the Brethren settlements were frequently out of touch with the centers of Brethren culture in the East. They were therefore more vulnerable to the thinning out of religious convictions and also to the loss of their German speech and cultural traits.

A hint of the troubles which were to come as the Brethren scattered over ever-greater distances is found in the minutes of the Annual Conferences of 1785 and 1790. During these years, much concern was expressed over the tendencies in the church on the distant frontier of the South Branch of the Potomac. The leaders of this congregation sought from the Conference a greater flexibility in the doctrine of nonresistance. They were unsuccessful—with the result that this church was lost to the

Brethren.

From 1794 to 1800, more serious problems were disturbing the doctrinal order of the churches in North Carolina. Extensive deviations were being noted in the refusal of the church there to practice disciplinary measures such as excommunication and avoidance of contact with members under the ban. Many also refused to believe in heaven, hell, and the wrath of God. Eventually, several of these congregations merged into the Universalist movement.

Around 1826, all of the churches of Kentucky, consisting of perhaps fifteen hundred members (Flory, 1932, page 29) were excommunicated. Differences had developed in the way that feetwashing and the love feast were conducted.[8] Trouble continued, however, because these sincere Brethren refused to consider themselves excommunicated. Rather, many of them moved to Illinois and continued to work in the churches. Finally, around 1855-1856, partly because of the powerful influence of Elder George Wolfe, a compromise was reached and the Far Western Brethren were conserved to the church.

It is interesting to note that in this instance a degree of divergence in doctrine and practice was tolerated. Annual Conference did not reject the committee's report which permitted differences in the order of the love feast and feetwashing to continue (Kurtz, 1867, page 108).

It would be helpful to summarize the period from 1780 to 1850. First, we note from the minutes of the Annual Conference that a large proportion of concern was expanded in keeping peace and order among the churches. Annual Conference had become a unifying and sanctioning instrument which served as a means of maintaining communication, building friendships, and preserving agreement among the increasingly scattered churches. It is quite likely that without this means the denomination would have been more greatly

---

[8]For a discussion of these doctrinal differences, see Flory, 1932, pages 31-35. The Far Western Brethren practiced the single mode of feetwashing, which was adopted as the official mode in the Annual Conference of 1919. During the eighteenth and nineteenth centuries, the double mode was accepted as correct by Annual Conference. The double mode involved the washing of the feet of several persons by a single individual.

fragmented than it was. With this in mind, it may be important to assess the many values which Annual Conferences have for the church today.

Second, we may feel somewhat impatient over the tendency of the church of this period to stress legalism and conformity in minute matters of belief and practice. This reflects a sharp contrast to today. We have departed far from the legalistic emphases on conformity. Now, we are much more open to accepting religious differences within the church and across denominational lines. We shall see that great stress on various kinds of religious conformity continued during the latter half of the nineteenth century. We shall see also that the church lost this struggle at several levels. One price of this continued emphasis was the division of the church into three fragments.

Developments Affecting Brethren Thought from 1860 to 1910

The sincerity with which the church held to its pacifist position was again severely tested during the Civil War. Rufus Bowman has stated that the church was firmly united in its opposition to war during this period. As in the Revolutionary War, especially as conditions worsened, few non-Brethren were sympathetic with the refusal of the Brethren to fight. D. P. Sayler, John Kline, and many other leaders were active in communicating and negotiating with government and military officials to obtain acceptable conditions for their constituencies. Because of their antislavery stand[9] and the tendency to regard the South as being in rebellion against the legitimate governmental authority, Brethren south of the Mason-Dixon Line bore an extra burden, suffering economic loss and severe alienation in their communities. Brethren families in the North also suffered economic losses and disfavor in their communities, but they did not bear the added stigma of their an-

---

[9]Since 1782 the church had been on record as officially forbidding slaveholding among the membership under penalty of excommunication, thus testifying at an early date to the strong conviction of the wrongness of this well-established social institution.

tislavery stand. Elder John Kline of Broadway, Virginia, was murdered for his forthright position against the war.

Although during this period draftees were permitted to pay a military tax of several hundred dollars in lieu of military service, many non-Brethren felt that this was getting off too easily. Some Brethren men were sent to prison. Others fled from their home states to escape persecution. During this era, the church remained firmly united in its conviction that the war was contrary to God's will. The theme of obedience to God's Word was strongly upheld. Those who wore the uniform and fought were excommunicated by rule of Annual Conference.

Other developments were presenting serious problems to the church during this period. Industrialization of the economy began to make available vast numbers of "worldly" products, many of which were regarded by the conservative elders as "sinful contraptions." During the Conferences between 1850 and 1900 much time was taken up with questions concerning the morality of cameras, lightning rods, store-bought clothes, carpets, musical instruments in home and church, jewelry, insurance, and many other items. The membership was more widely spread and less closely knit. Consequently, there was greater tendency for members to become identified with those who were described as "worldly" people and to practice customs which were "strange" to the ways of the "old Brethren." During this period, excommunication continued to be practiced against flagrant nonconformists.

While many of these concerns may appear to us now as quite peripheral to the faith, the real significance of these issues pertained to the problem of maintaining a high order of loyalty to more basic Brethren values of faithfulness to Christ and pious living. Conformity of the members to numerous restrictive regulations on personal conduct, mode of dress, house furnishing, etc., was taken to represent inner spiritual health, unity with the Brethren, and willingness to submit obediently to the will of God. They functioned effectively also to keep clear lines of demarcation between the people of God and the unregenerate. The Brethren deeply prized their religious values and the church. Most were willing to observe "outward" as well as "inward" conformity to the demands of the spiritual authority they accepted. In the closely knit agricultural communities, they were also economically and socially dependent upon one another. Consequently, the church's sanctions were usually effective. Few options outside the church seemed viable to them. Under these circumstances, the sectarian and Germanic character of the Brethren was preserved against weakening longer than would otherwise have been possible.

At the same time that the products and the social modifications of industrialization were producing many new strains and conflicts within the church, other developments were coming to affect the denomination. Printing and publications, although opposed at first, soon began to become popular avenues of communication.

The Brethren "theologian" of the nineteenth century, Peter Nead, was writing and publishing books of which his *Theological Writings* (1850) was most famous. In his work, Nead sought to conserve the traditional doctrinal emphases of the Brethren. Although reared a Lutheran, he became deeply committed to the Dunker view of the church. His first publication, expressing a central doctrine of Mack, was entitled *Primitive Christianity;* it was published in 1833.

In 1851, Henry Kurtz, a brilliant and intellectually aggressive man, began publishing a religious paper called the *Gospel Visitor* (from it *Messenger,* familiar to us today, is descended). In 1867, Kurtz published, against considerable opposition, a compilation of Conference minutes *(The Brethren's Encyclopedia)* with his own personal commentary.

The *Gospel Visitor* took a moderate position with respect to the massive changes which were beginning to develop in the denomination. Consequently, Kurtz's paper gained wide support and influence. Meanwhile, a small group of members were seeking more radical changes and reforms in the church. They were not satisfied to go slowly. One of their spokesmen, Henry R. Holsinger, began publication in 1864 of a paper (the *Christian Family Companion*) which became a rallying point for an increasingly active progressive agitation. The conservative membership was soon served with its own paper, the *Vin-*

dicator, which was started at Dayton, Ohio, by Samuel Kinsey in 1870. The publishers of these papers sought to create sentiment and support for their respective causes.

By this time three well-defined factions had emerged in the church, each seeking to promote its own view and to manipulate Annual Conference policy.[10] Among the changes to which the conservative faction were most opposed were the running of Sunday schools and educational institutions, conducting revivals, changing the mode of feetwashing, payment of ministers, and departures from the prescribed order of dress.[11] After the Conference of 1881, around four thousand members split away and organized the Old Order German Baptist Church. Today this group, still clinging to the old ways, maintains a membership of around five thousand.

The progressive faction sought many changes in policy and practice and were often intemperate in their attacks. In 1882, Annual Conference disfellowshiped Holsinger and some of his followers. These in turn sought reconciliation and a return to the church but were unsuccessful. In 1883, they organized separately with a membership of perhaps five thousand, calling themselves the Progressive Brethren Church. Their growth has been modest.

The remaining Brethren, numbering around 55,000, experienced a rapid growth and prosperity in the years after 1880. The troublesome controversies and disagreements over doctrines and practices were reduced. The church turned

---

[10]For a discussion of these developments, see J. S. Flory, *Flashlights From History,* Brethren Publishing House, 1932, Chapters X-XII.

[11]During the nineteenth century, plain dressing in accordance with a standard called "the garb" was enforced as a major form of obedience to God's Word. The verse of scripture, "Be ye not conformed to this world," was taken to mean that one should dress differently from worldly people. Uniformity in dress for both men and women was stressed. The form of the dress was determined by custom and set forth in the minutes of Annual Conference. The dress question was dealt with a total of more than seventy-five times between 1800 and 1916. The prayer veil worn by the women was an especially important requirement relating to the status of women in the church as taught by St. Paul. For a nostalgic discussion of these matters, consult Mallott, 1954, Chapters 27, 28.

its interests outward into missionary activities and to growing enterprises at home such as the schools and the colleges.

The educational movement played a significant role in the tensions and the developments of the period. Of course, the Old Order faction had opposed innovations such as Sunday schools, academies, and colleges. Nevertheless, they spread rapidly between 1860 and 1880. After the removal of the Old Order group, energy and funds found their way more enthusiastically into the educational movement. Many colleges—far too many for so small a membership—were begun only to fail. A few survived to prosper and exert important influences of the thought-ways and patterns of the life of the church in succeeding years. At the present time, six colleges are Brethren related. They are Bridgewater, Elizabethtown, Juniata, Manchester, McPherson, and La Verne.

The colleges and Bethany Seminary have served through the years to prepare for Christian service a large body of teachers, ministers, and missionaries. These were frequently outstanding individuals in their areas of service, bringing respect and honor upon their churches. The colleges have also served as one of several media by which scientific modes of thought and liberalizing ideas have penetrated the church from the great universities.

The Modern Period in Brethren Thought

The last sixty to seventy years have witnessed a truly remarkable transformation in the church's life and thought. Only convenience and the occurrence of drastic changes in the Church of the Brethren permit us to consider this lengthy and complicated period under a single caption. A definitive treatment of our topic would certainly require much more in the way of space and treatment.

A hint of the changing of values is found in the 1911 minutes of Annual Conference, which dealt extensively with the dress question. Up to this time, it was clearly understood that those refusing to dress in accord with the strict regulations called "the order" or "the garb" were to be excommunicated. The 1911 Conference accepted a report which stressed continued teaching concerning the order of dress but seemed not to specify clearly the excommunication of those who depart from the order. With the weakening of the penalty against failure to follow the order, the next fifteen or twenty years saw the marked decline of this universally distinctive aspect of Brethren life. By 1925, the wearing of the garb was primarily a voluntary matter among the laity of most congregations.

The gradual change in thought involved in these developments is the growth of the conviction that the Bible teaches general principles pertaining to simple and godly dress, and not a rigid code.[12] This argument had long been heard among the Brethren. Now, after around 1920, it came to be widely held. The revised statement of Brethren doctrine (*The Brethren's Card*), presented to the Conference of 1922 but not officially adopted, makes no mention of either excommunication or the dress. The Brethren were turning away from the legalism of and the stress on outward appearance which characterized them in the nineteenth century. Perhaps even more important, the exercising of disciplinary action was declining. Because of these subtle changes, a small group of conservatives broke away in 1926, calling themselves the Dunkard Brethren. They sought to escape what they regarded as growing "worldliness" in the church—meaning the spread of life insurance, the paid ministry, neckties, the use of musical instruments in worship, and similar matters.

A new emphasis was growing in Protestantism in the 1920s. Sometimes called the "social gospel," it stressed the view that the social order and its problems ought to become for the Christian church a focus of major concern. Identified with the liberal wing of Protestantism and naively optimistic about the ultimate transformation of society into a Christian order, it was attractive to many Brethren members. It presented an opportunity for many Brethren to enlarge their concern beyond

[12]For a discussion of the development of the doctrine of the simple life during this period, see Emmert F. Bittinger, "The Simple Life: A Chapter in the Evolution of a Doctrine," *(Brethren Life and Thought,* Vol. XXIII, No. 2, Spring 1978, pp. 104-114).

the narrow limits of sectarian and localized problems. It represented another expression of the desire of the church to turn in mission to the world.

Also during the period from 1920 to 1940 the ministry underwent a significant redefinition in the denomination. The free ministry conducted by unpaid ministers called by their local churches to work in a largely unspecialized and non-professional role was gradually giving way to a new kind of clergy. The ministry came toward the end of this period to be redefined as consisting of full-time, paid clergymen who had received college and seminary educations. They became more set apart from the laity by virtue of educational training and growing professionalism. The role and the significance of the lay minister has continued to recede in importance and meaning. One aspect of this decline of the free ministry and its lessened significance in the church was the decision of Annual Conference in 1967 to eliminate entirely the eldership as a third degree of the ministry and to discontinue the elders' body as an organized entity.

By the end of World War II, American life in general had undergone transformation, and so had that of the Brethren. The strongholds of rural conservatism were being effectively counterbalanced by an increasingly urbanized and progressive membership. Universal public education was adding its impact to the influences of the family and home. Radio, television, and other news media brought the world into the living room. The crucial and disturbing social issues of war and peace, race relations, drug addiction, the sexual revolution, riots and demonstrations, urban decay, and the world population explosion began to take the stage of Brethren thought.

How could the church ever have been so upset about the issues of neckties, insurance, photographs, carpets, and musical instruments? These concerns were a distortion of the Pietistic heritage in a denomination whose cultural and social isolation had cut it off from the outside world. Between 1945 and 1982 the church became thoroughly Americanized and joined many of its major ideas and concerns with those of the country as a whole.

The Brethren were attempting to fill a new place in the nation and the world. They discovered their common cause with other denominations. This development is well shown by active involvement in high levels with the national and world councils of churches and the exchange of visits with the Russian Orthodox Church. Ecumenicity was further expressed in the cooperation of denominations and clergy at the community level. Having discovered our common Christian ground with other religious bodies, some were willing to explore the possibility of organic union as well as mere cooperation. As seen in the Annual Conference of 1966, when the delegates voted against official participation in the Consultation on Church Union, many still felt a strong identity with our heritage and feared losing any remaining distinctive aspects of our church and its ministry to the world.

One may well inquire what remains of our distinctive heritage! And indeed this deserves thoughtful consideration and self-examination by the Brethren of today. Some may well argue that the church has lost only its irrelevant distinctions and shackles from the past. The church has come into the world to minister more fully in times like this. This is a well-turned argument—but not one to be lightly given and soon forgotten! It is one that requires more work and sacrifice than we have thus far been willing to give.

Nevertheless, new ministries and new applications of old Brethren themes are still vitally alive among us. They have possibilities which are yet unrealized. Let us trace one of these.

Obedience to Christ found new expression among the Brethren in World War II. In 1945, the Annual Conference heard it reported that among the young men of the church 1,424 were noncombatants, 1,386 were in civilian public service, and fourteen were in prison because of their refusal to bear arms. Perhaps only about ten percent of the Brethren men chose to refuse to participate in military activities, but at least the spirit of obedience was still alive and strong in the church. The tremendous outpouring of money and personnel at great sacrifice in support of Civilian Public Service was truly remarkable. It tesified to the unity of the church and to its loyalty to its ancient belief in the wrongness of war.

Even more encouraging, these young men and the

denomination were not satisfied with a merely negative witness against war. The desire to express Christian obedience in meaningful service touched a responsive cord. The central idea of civilian public service was to demonstrate love by performing some kind of work which would be consistent with the way of Christ. No payment of a tax in lieu of military service could satisfy this desire for a positive witness to the gospel!

The suffering engendered by the world's most costly war brought to the surface of Brethren life not only revulsion against war but also the desire to relieve suffering. The Brethren Service ministry greatly expanded during the war until it became a major arm of the church. The movement went forward under the stimulus of the familiar verse, "Inasmuch as you did it unto one of these my Brethren, even the least, you did it unto me" (Matthew 25:40). The myrtlewood cup of service became a familiar symbol in most places of worship.

The report of this ministry in 1948 reveals active programs to minister to human need in ten foreign countries with strong supporting operations at New Windsor, Nappanee, and other places in the States. During the same year the Heifer Project shipped 1,807 animals to European countries in a postwar ministry.

The world-directed ministry did not cease at the end of the war. Vast amounts of money continued to be expended in Brethren Service into the 1950s and the 1960s. Furthermore, a new avenue of service was taken up by the youth of the church and came to be known as Brethren Volunteer Service.[13] Through this ministry, which continues to the present, several thousand young men and women have sought to express their faithfulness and concern for a broken world through a variety of practical ministries. A new generation of Brethren were fulfilling their obedience to Christ, turning to the world with their dollars and their lives.[14]

---

[13]The creativity and the success of this program is attested by the fact that it became one of several youth service programs studied by the federal government as a source of ideas for the Peace Corps.

[14]For a detailed discussion of the social service programs of the church, see Roger E. Sappington, *Brethren Social Policy* (The Brethren Press, Elgin, Ill., 1961).

Concern for the world was not new among the Brethren, but it was finding new modes of fulfillment. The expression of obedience in the nineteenth century took the form of nonconformity to the world and to strict legalistic submission to scriptural commands pertaining to church ordinances, the garb, and the simple life. In the latter half of the twentieth century, the conscious call of the church was to turn to the world. Reconciliation and the relevancy of the church to the needs of the modern church member *and* his society became familiar themes. The urge toward involvement caused reevaluation of the effectiveness of the traditional, institution-centered programs. It was said by many of the younger and more action-oriented members that a world deep in the crises of moral and social disorder must not find the church standing idly by keeping house, performing rituals, and conducting a self-centered ministry. The forms of these new ministries are taking shape. The focus of concern by the church on crucial moral issues vital to the individual and his social order holds the promise of stimulating the development of new expressions of the old Brethren theme of obedience and service to Christ.

The direction and the quality of this obedience seem already to be clearly determined by the trends of the recent past. It is an obedience which arises out of the attitude of compassion and love which is at the heart of the New Testament image of Christ. It is an obedience which goes beyond the letter to the spirit of Jesus. It does not neglect its own members, but it is not limited in concern to the faithful. Not a ministry which subordinates all other values to the salvation of the soul in the hereafter, it concentrates on the condition of man in his contemporary ordeal. The whole person, and not just his soul, becomes the object of Christ's reconciliation and redemption—in the family, the factory, the slum, and the school.

The Pietism of the Schwarzenau Brethren was founded on the vital and renewing experience of the Holy Spirit in the inner man. It expressed itself in a form of obedience which represented a clear-cut challenge to the Christianity of the eighteenth century. It was involved in the religious and social issues of its day. The witness was against the empty formalism of the established churches and the immorality of both the clergy and the laity.

One aspect of the Pietism active among the Brethren to-day is the sensitivity to the call to be obedient to the spirit of Christ as it finds application in the urgent, contemporary human setting. The servant role of the church and the compassionate ministries to the human condition in the manner of the good Samaritan and the cleansing of the temple are increasingly exemplary of the Brethren in the twentieth century. Effective protest and constructive action against social, economic, personal, and political injustices—including war—continue to mark our denomination. Today, the opportunity still exists for our church to lead Christendom into new directions and creative ministries. As Brethren today, do we need to take our calling more seriously and respond more radically in our commitment and obedience?

5

The Lifestyle of the Brethren

Prologue

Our examination of the Brethren would be incomplete and one-sided if we did not turn to their way of life. The discussions relating to the geographical spread of the church and the development of its doctrines did not completely exclude *some glimpses* into the topic to be treated in this chapter. Certainly they did not provide us with an extended treatment of this intriguing aspect of our common heritage. This question well deserves a special chapter for its consideration.

It is not an easy task to define the Brethren style of life. This phrase, however, has so many connotations and is used in so many connections that an attempt to define it is necessary.

Style of life usually is taken to reflect important orientations and attitudes of an individual or a group. The values to which one is committed emerge in daily activity and in the allocation of time, energy, and resources. Decisions which are made mirror these attitudes. Life ambitions center around them. Therefore, the lifestyle of the Brethren shall refer to those stable patterns of day-to-day activity in the home, the church, and the community. It is in these areas that the deepest and most important life commitments and attitudes work themselves out into self-expression.

It would be dangerously easy to fall into the error of thinking that the lifestyle of the Brethren is the perfect mirror-image of our church doctrines and religious values. There is never a perfect correspondence of the ideal with the actual—even among our revered forebears. Actions never quite fulfill intentions, and high ideals are always considerably out of reach. We shall not be disappointed, however, in our search for a good measure of consistency in Brethren ideals and practice. The Brethren of a former generation did well in this respect. We shall be greatly interested also in assessing the question of whether *our* lifestyle as Christians is as consistent today with our ideals as was true in the past. Perhaps we cannot expect to reach conclusions which would represent a very high degree of consensus among readers. Nevertheless, we should not sidestep the question of whether our lifestyle today is consistent with our proclaimed values.

If in our survey we discover that our way of life—either past or present—deviates markedly from the religious values which we proclaim, how shall this be regarded? Shall it suffice to label these deviations as hypocritical and continue to reassert our verbalized allegiance to the values of the past? If our way of life has changed markedly, shall this be seen *only* in relation to ancient values in our religious heritage? Large areas of inconsistency with older values indicate the emergence of *new* values, not merely departure from the ancient. We would do well to recognize this. The focus then can be placed in part upon these emerging values. Do they represent a more relevant application of the same biblical principles from which Mack and his associates drew the values meaningful in their time? Can the current life patterns of the Brethren be seen as a contemporary expression of biblical principles? Or, are the life patterns espoused by the present generation to be seen as a rejection of biblical principles? Even more pertinent, have these new patterns arisen without reference to them? Does our way of life today represent an uncritical acceptance of contemporary culture and the values and ideals which underlie it?

These questions deserve serious thought today. They will not readily be answered. If Brethren can come to grips with these issues it is possible that they will find a new avenue of meaningful ministry to people seeking to find fulfillment in a world very different from that of Alexander Mack.

The life ways of a people rarely arise out of rational planning or conscious determination. Rather, they appear as habitual or preferred modes of conduct which resolve practical problems of survival and maintenance. If the beliefs and the commitments of the people are strong, their day-by-day life will tend to be more or less consistently patterned around them. Work, play, family, community, and religious life will take a form which reflects the dominant values. In our denomination, these primary ideals have been simplicity, integrity, community, piety, humility, service, obedience, faithfulness, and nonviolence. Other values such as frugality, hard work, and nonconformity to the world have also been upheld.

Other than religious forces have been important in forming the life patterns of the Brethren. Among these, the first to come to mind are the Germanic background, the harsh conditions of the American frontier, and the rural-farm heritage. Others were operative also, and we shall have occasion to refer to them.

Family Life Patterns

The family customs of a people are among their most important social institutions. This is true because the basic cultural values and norms which are present in all socialized adults (in this instance, parents) are most readily learned by children in the intimate, emotionalized relationships of the family setting. Some of these patterns are consciously taught and enforced by parents. Many of them, however, are learned in more subtle ways. The growing child tends to respond to people around him by thinking and behaving in ways which reduce his tensions and which are rewarding to him. Fortunately for the sake of cultural continuity of the group, the vast majority of these learning experiences result in the effective transmission of the desired behavioral patterns from one generation to the next.

Culture is not transferred from old to young without modification, and of course culture is continually changing in one way or another. Prior to the industrial revolution which struck the Brethren in the midnineteenth century, life patterns were changing more slowly than now. People tended toward conservatism, and maintenance of the old ways was more successful. During the recent decades, cultural, social, and economic movement has been greatly increased. It is no longer feasible or possible for all of the family patterns appropriate to the early nineteenth century to be maintained or transmitted. Our purpose will be to examine family life prior to the industrial revolution, to trace some of the changes, and to raise issues concerning these trends.[1]

The early Brethren family was strongly rural and farm based. It possessed quite a different economic system and division of labor. Its social life centered in the family, the church, and the exchange of family visits among kin and other Brethren. Transportation was by foot or horse-drawn vehicles. Ankrum (1962, page 70) tells the story of Barbara Garber of the Flat Rock congregation in the Shenandoah Valley of Virginia, who, on several occasions, walked to visit relatives in Maryland and Pennsylvania, a total round-trip distance of four hundred miles. Visits any great distance from the homestead were rare and were usually undertaken only because of necessity.

Economically, the early family was a productive unit and therefore more independent. Most of the food, clothes, and household necessities were produced directly on the farm or in the neighborhood. Many crafts were known by adults. Fathers taught them to their sons in the process of daily operation of the farm and the household. Shoes were homemade. Even many of the household furnishings were made on the farm. Mothers taught essential activities: sewing, weaving, gardening, cooking, preserving food, and many other crafts upon which survival and prosperity were dependent. Each farm had a small orchard, more than likely possessing a large variety of fruit trees. Bush fruits too were highly prized, and wild fruits, berries, and nuts served to give variety and quality to the diet. Domesticated animals added necessary protein to the diet.

---

[1]Earlier studies which treat this topic in some detail are: F. D. Dove, *Cultural Changes in the Church of the Brethren*, Brethren Publishing House, 1932; J. H. Ziegler, *The Broken Cup*, Brethren Publishing House, 1942; and E. F. Bittinger, "The Church-Family Relationship in the Church of the Brethren Across Two Centuries," 1951 (unpublished Master of Arts dissertation, University of Maryland).

Cattle were seldom killed for food because of the difficulty of preserving the meat. Pork was smoked and salted and thus easily preserved. Wild meat was also commonly used.

At this point the reader might be reminded that all of these—and other essential farm and household duties too numerous to mention—required a vast amount of work. Each person was busy from dawn to dark. To have families with many children was an economic advantage. Consequently, large families were desirable and envied. They meant prosperity to the family. More fields could be cleared and cultivated. More food could be grown. The wife and mother had many hands to help her with her numerous tasks.

In accord with the biblical principle that the father is the head of the wife and to be obeyed by the children—a tradition greatly stressed in the patriarchal family system of Germany from which the Brethren came—the father kept strict order and permitted no deviation from the rules he laid down. Any spirit of disobedience on the part of the children was punished. Other attitudes taught were submissiveness, self-control, honesty, modesty, and respectfulness. Today's miniskirts, lipstick, and costume jewelry would have scandalized the church, requiring excommunication or public confession.

Hard work was valued not only for its product but also for its own sake as a virtue. Frugality was taught and observed because it was consistent with the high price in time and skill which was required to earn money or to make the essentials of everyday existence. Goods were not wasted since they represented value easily understood by child and adult alike.

In the rural farm family of the past, the sense of belonging was strong and enduring. Emotional bonds were built up and characterized family relations during the entire lifetime. Group values and goals took priority over those of the individual. The family welfare as a whole was of first concern. The role of the individual member was evaluated in relation to this. Family visiting was frequent and an annual clan reunion was a major event. Father and sons often farmed cooperatively, providing each other with extra labor when needed. Sons often received assistance from the family when setting up farms for themselves. While sons and daughters remained at home, income and property belonged to the family group with little development of a sense of individual ownership. Under these conditions, insurance was deemed unnecessary. In time of catastrophe, neighbors and kin were ready to assist.

In addition to having many children, the Brethren family was typically increased in size by the presence of grandparents and sometimes unmarried or widowed uncles and aunts and other relatives who needed care and a family. Few people lived alone apart from families. Care of the handicapped and the aged was accepted as a joyous and binding obligation upon the children. For parents to have to go to the "poor house" or county home brought a feeling of disgrace and humiliation upon the children.

Matters pertaining to sex were seldom discussed because they were unmentionable, secretive, and ambiguous in religious meaning. It is doubtful that sex education of the young was extensive or even thought necessary. In the farm environment children were apt observers. They certainly were not ignorant of the biological elements of sex. On the other hand, in an atmosphere of religious repression of sex feelings, the wife could scarcely cultivate any desire for sexual fulfillment. A sense of guilt possibly surrounded such feelings. Any talk of sex usually related to misbehavior and took on a tone of gossip.

Recreation and leisure for the adults were not elaborate. While Sunday was a day of rest, it was not consumed in commercial recreation or games. Youth and adults found social outlets in visiting with other families and in church attendance where extensive socializing took place.

The rule against divorce was one of the most strictly enforced in the church. Marriage was regarded as permanent before God. Writing in the late nineteenth century, D. L. Miller said, "The Brethren hold that the marriage bond can be dissolved only by death. Divorce and remarriage are practically unknown among the membership"[2] Henry Kurtz (1867, page 90) stated that divorce might be permitted in exceptional cases where adultery has been committed, but that the inno-

---

[2]D. L. Miller, "The Brethren or Dunkards," p. 10 in *Brethren's Tracts and Pamphlets*, Vol. 1, Mount Morris, Illinois: Brethren Publishing Co., 1889.

cent party must not remarry. Divorce could never take place with a view of remarriage.

Marriage of young people out of the church was also frowned upon. Strong parental and church controls were built up to prevent it. Gillin (1906, page 74) refers to the hostile attitude of the church from early times down to the present to marriage with anyone outside the Dunker Church. Given the very strong in-group feelings within the church, the tendency was to believe that other denominations were in grave error before God. Since they desired to keep kin and group ties intact, it was altogether natural for the Brethren to place high value upon marriage within the church social group.

Prayer and Bible reading had a prominent place among family activities. The home was the major educational agency, and it carried the major role in religious training, too. Regular family worship was a part of the family ideal. That this custom sometimes degenerated into a chore or an empty ritual is indicated by the following description of a family altar around 1895.

> We had it at night. Father would sit around and read until he would get sleepy. None of us children were permitted to go to bed until we had family worship. We would get sleepy and lie down and go to sleep. Then when father was ready to go to bed we would all be waked up for family worship. Father would read and then pray. Several times he went to sleep while praying (Ziegler, 1942, page 105).

Ziegler's study indicates that around eighty-two percent of the older Brethren men he interviewed had family altar regularly in their homes as children.

It would be unfair to leave the impression that the family altar was not meaningful. Carried out in a creative way, it had significant religious value. A prized possession of the author is the ancient leatherbound German Testament which his great-great-grandfather, Peter Fike of Eglon, West Virginia, customarily carried to the fields along with the farm tools he used. The father of five sons and eight daughters, he would read to them and tell Bible stories on work breaks and in the evenings. The quality of religious commitment of this family is attested by the fact that well over one hundred ministers can be counted among the descendants and husbands of descendants of Peter Fike today. He served sixty years in the ministry and in his prime traveled as many as fifteen hundred miles a year in his work. Even at the age of ninety to ninety-five he kept regular preaching appointments at Brookside, walking three miles each way to conduct the Sunday services.

The Church and Worship

Brethren church houses expressed in their architecture certain important values. In prosperous and substantial communities they were simply but sturdily built. Heavy walls of stone or brick spoke of permanence and stability. Usually rectangular in shape, they gave no impression of churchliness or display. Those built before the era of Sunday schools contained only a single large room with perhaps an attic in which those who came great distances to attend the love feast might sleep. Occasionally a sideroom would accommodate a substantial brick bake oven and a stove for preparing meals.

The interior arrangements would be indeed strange to many younger Brethren today. The unencumbered preachers' table was placed along the side of the rectangular interior against a plain, undecorated wall. Typically, there was no pulpit or raised platform for the speaker. Instead, there was a long table behind which the ministers—perhaps as many as ten, with their long, flowing beards—sat facing the congregation. The ministers were not elevated by a platform because the distinctions between the ministers and the laity in origin, status, and training were minimized. In Europe and in the early period in America, ministers were called teachers or exhorters. Their role was not that of the clergymen in the state churches. They typically received no pay for their work and they supported themselves and their families by their regular occupations as farmers or craftsmen.

In some instances, each end of the sanctuary was inclined so as to raise the pews in order that the minister could be better observed.[3] This also permitted the young people and nonmembers to be watched by the congregation on the main floor—a practical means of maintaining good behavior! These church buildings almost invariably had at least two entrances. One corresponded to the side of the church in which the women sat and the other to the men's side. Movement in and out of the church was minimized by the embarrassment of walking in and out on either side of the ministers and their table, which was frequently located between the doors along the side. Pews were plain and homemade. They were designed to be sufficiently comfortable to serve their purpose but not so comfortable as to encourage sleep. Windows were of clear glass since stained glass was too worldly and was reminiscent of high church traditions.

The services would be regarded as long by today's standards. Often several ministers preached during a service. A minister might speak up to an hour or longer, usually without benefit of written notes. Use of notes would be taken to indicate lack of response to the leading of the Spirit. Hymns were sung slowly with a breath taken between every few words. The singing was unaccompanied by instruments since the organ and the piano were considered worldly and pretentious. The hymn leader would "line out"[4] the words of the hymn, a procedure necessitated by the scarcity of hymnbooks and by ancient custom. Services were typically in the German language up to 1850 in the East, with some congregations in Pennsylvania continuing the German language services well into the twentieth century.

Prayers, as well as sermons, were long, sometimes lasting twenty to thirty minutes. The congregation invariably knelt with knees on the hard floor. To the middle aged and the elderly, the prayer was a test of physical as well as spiritual stamina. To the young, the prayer was anticipated as a period

---

[3]An example is the Beaver Run church house in West Virginia, whose origin goes back to 1785 when the Arnolds and the Leathermans moved into the Patterson Creek area. Their present church house was built in 1876.

[4]The leader recited a line or two before the congregation, which then sang them.

of whispering, visiting, and occasionally uncontrollable giggling. Prior to and following the services, the customary exchange of the "holy kiss" was observed, being practiced, of course, only among those of the same sex.

The love feast, practiced once or twice a year, was one of the most important occasions. All members in good standing were expected to be present. To be absent without good cause would imply that one was disgruntled or out of fellowship with the church. Prior to the time of the love feast, the deacons were required by sacred custom to visit every member of the congregation in order to determine whether each was in full fellowship with the church. Communion might be delayed until the deacons' visitation was completed. Not only did the membership of the congregation attend, but many families came from neighboring churches—both Brethren and non-Brethren.

Because of the practice of "closed communion," non-Brethren could not participate though they were welcome to observe. Sometimes special preaching services were held for the large crowds of non-Brethren present. Building and grounds were taxed to their full to accommodate all the people. Non-members were accustomed to attending Sunday services and the love feasts because they were significant social occasions to young and old alike. Frequently, as many people were present on the grounds as were found inside the crowded church house. This was one of the few times that youth could find to be together without being under constant surveillance by their parents. The grounds and the roads would be covered with buggies and horses parked wherever there was a bit of space.[5]

Church organization was simple, consisting primarily of the positions of minister, elder, and deacon. In later years, a secretary would take minutes of the church council, which was

[5]Some records from the Beaver Run church, Hampshire County, West Virginia, throw light on our topic. "To give an idea of the number of people who attended Love Feast sixty years ago, the following list of supplies is taken from an old Minute Book: 57 lbs. butter, 95 loaves of bread, 100 lbs. of meat, 8 gal. applebutter, 8 lbs. coffee. One year the bread numbered 141 loaves" (Bittinger 1945, page 45).

ideally run in a democratic fashion. Trustees were needed only to fulfill a legal requirement of holding the title to church property. Special committees were formed temporarily to carry out specific assignments such as building or remodeling a church house or visiting some brother or sister who was thought to be deviating in some belief or in behavior. An important function of the council meeting was the maintenance of strict conformity with church practices by disciplining the careless or the disobedient. Such persons frequently were required to confess sins before the congregation and to promise not to engage in such behavior again. These sanctions served to keep clear and unambiguous the exact limits of behavior not tolerated. Furthermore, it kept the membership behaviorally and doctrinally uniform, since those unwilling to submit to the Brethren pattern were disfellowshiped or withdrew voluntarily.

Annual Conference served for congregations and districts a role similar to that of local councils to individual members. The Annual Conference was the highest authority in the church. Its definitions of moral and doctrinal values served as a standard for the entire denomination, though departure from its pronouncements was not uncommon.

The rural community social organization also contributed to the nature of the Brethren life patterns in the nineteenth century. Primitive forms of transportation and communication kept people closer to their homes and restricted their opportunities for enduring contact with differing lifestyles and ideas. A family was more intimately in contact with nearby neighbors and Brethren families. Interdependence of neighbors extended not only to the exchange of labor and economic goods in face-to-face relations but included also the need for social esteem and respect from those upon whom one was dependent and in continual contact. One's reputation was known and continually evaluated, and there was no escape into anonymity or impersonal relations. Every family's participation in the intimate relations comprising each of the overlapping economic, social, and religious systems which made up the community, kept up a heavy pressure to conform to accepted standards in the respective spheres. These same relationships, however, provided a solid basis for meeting the social, economic, and spiritual needs of the people in a satisfying and effective way.

Brethren were forbidden to belong to lodges and fraternal societies. Furthermore, voluntary organizations and clubs were uncommon in the early or middle nineteenth century. Fairs and carnivals were not only infrequent but were also tabooed. Cooperative activities involving the exchange of labor in times of harvest, butchering, or house- and barn-building provided enjoyable social occasions and strengthened the sense of unity and mutual obligation among neighbors.

The strong feeling of mutual obligation and loyalty was widely extended to apply not only to Brethren families but also to non-Brethren families and to neighbors in the community. Thus if the husband or the wife in a family fell ill, neighbors would take whatever time was needed away from their own work to gather at the farm or the home of the ill person to get the work done. If a new house or barn was to be built, this often called for a special kind of community cooperative effort called a "house raising" or a "barn raising." Large numbers of people voluntarily donated one or more days of work at such times, knowing that such work was appreciated and often reciprocated when the opportunity arose. If a house or a barn burned, such cooperative occasions were all the more likely and even more meaningful to all concerned.

Because they lived in closely knit agricultural communities in which losses of time and property due to causes such as fire, accident, and illness, were softened and alleviated by the support of neighbors and friends, the Brethren at first resisted the purchase of insurance. At one level, they saw insurance as a threat to the moral and economic integration of the community as expressed in mutual aid. However, most opposition to fire insurance (also to lightning rods) centered on the belief that one should put his chief trust in God. Fire insurance was considered by Annual Conference in 1847, 1875, and 1879. The purchasing of such insurance was not forbidden as long as it was "done in a mutual way," indicating a continued strong adherence to the principle of mutual aid. Life insurance, however, was strictly prohibited for many years and did not come into wide use until well into the twentieth century.

Mutual aid at butchering time is worthy of special comment since this social institution is rapidly disappearing because of both the widespread growth of small specialized butchering services in agricultural communities and the declining use of pork. Although mutual aid at butchering time began to decline in the Middletown Valley of Maryland in the 1950s, the Harry Sowers family was one of the last to give it up. When the time came for the killing of some six or eight large hogs, neighbors and the pastors of the three local churches of the community were invited to help.

Activities began around seven o'clock in the morning after the regular farm chores were completed. All the hogs would be killed, scalded, scraped, hung, and drawn by eight or eight-thirty o'clock. The ten to fifteen men were efficient workers, and each knew his specialized task best. All heavy work was done by noon.

Meanwhile, the women folk, including the wives of the visiting farmers and ministers, were busily occupied also. Some were working outside cutting, scraping, washing, and processing the meat products. Another group prepared dinner for between thirty-five and fifty hungry people. The large dinner table accommodated between twelve and fifteen persons at a time, but there was no lingering there. It must serve three or four settings. A minister ate with each table. Although each minister had assisted with butchering since early morning, his special role at the dinner table was to offer a prayer. The dinner table was heavy with more than a dozen steaming dishes. In addition to fresh pork, there were several other kinds of meats. Sumptuous desserts followed the main part of the meal.

Such occasions not only served to get the work done efficiently, they also built a strong sense of community and assisted in the ability of each person to obtain a sense of identity and of belonging. Perhaps specialized butchering services are more convenient. However, they can never contribute to the social, religious, and moral integration of the community in the ways that the various forms of mutual aid did in the past. With the demise of these ancient social institutions, the people of the community obtain some of these same values from membership in civic clubs and other voluntary organizations.

A Changing Society and a Changing Lifestyle

In comparing the way of life of the Brethren a hundred twenty-five years ago with that which we know today, the reader has undoubtedly already been impressed with the fact that "things are different." In fact, they are so different that one wonders how the transformation could have taken place so rapidly. Of course, most of these changes are the direct consequence of massive changes in the entire fabric of American life. We cannot trace all the changes in American society and show how they each affected the church. A very brief picture in broad brush strokes will have to suffice in our limited space.

In the past hundred years, the American people have become urbanized in their way of life. Efficient farming through the use of machinery, hybrid seeds, fertilization, and effective management has changed our population from one which was ninety percent rural in 1790 to one which now exceeds seventy percent urban. Less than ten percent of our labor force now works on farms. The changes in the labor force required to produce manufactured products in great demand in our expanding economy have provided many people with specialized occupations unheard of a hundred years ago. To the westward migration was added a new population movement— one which took people into the cities and then into the suburbs.

The growth of learning in the colleges and the universities went hand in hand with the growth of science and its application to practical matters capable of producing an economic profit. With the invention of a national transportation system, manufactured products came to be distributed to the entire populace, thus inducing further economic growth. The automobile brought with it spatial mobility. Prosperity brought economic mobility. The radio, the movies, newspapers, and television stimulated a rapid mobility and diffusion of ideas. All forms of travel, education, and literature further increased the exposure of the population to new knowledge, patterns, norms, and values.

In 1882, with the church bereft of its balancing and restraining conservative wing, it was almost inevitable that the Brethren lifestyle would move toward the mainstream of American culture. The movement of the church was slow at first. But the merging of lifestyles was clearly recognized in the second and third decades of the twentieth century. Dove (1932, page 236), evaluating these trends in 1931, wrote, "The present cultural trends among the Brethren . . . reflect the influence of current social forces. The direction is toward the open road of modern culture." Ziegler (1942, page 165), writing twelve years later, also identified the trends of change. He predicted that the cultural markings on the cup of Brethren culture will scarcely be recognizable a hundred years from now. Robert Eshelman, analyzing the changing values of the Brethren, did not disagree with the foregoing conclusions. Writing in 1948, he said that "the prediction can be made that if the present trend continues, the Brethren will shift their values to the point of no longer being unique. The shift is not pronounced, however, and is not likely to increase radically in the immediate future . . . ." (Eshelman, 1948, page 229). The trends are discernible and definite. The only questions appear to be "Will the trends continue?" and "How long will it take?"

Perhaps few would desire to throw the trends of Brethren change in full reverse toward their original patterns. Rather, a more realistic concern might be to ask, "Which of the patterns and values of the Brethren have relevance today? Which ones speak to the needs of people in our time? How can these be encouraged and expanded in the contemporary church and society?"

The remainder of the chapter will be devoted to an attempt to answer, very inadequately to be sure, some of these questions as related to the family and the church.

Some Family Life Patterns Today

The Brethren family has undergone drastic modification. But it is not about to fall apart or disintegrate. As with the American family as a whole, it has responded to the changing times by adapting its structure and functions. It continues to meet the needs of its members. Indeed, it is doubtful that, without changing, it could have continued to satisfy the needs of the people as well as it does now. Any social institution which fails to serve the basic needs of its members is eventually doomed to disappear.

Today the family is smaller. While this has contributed to the decline in the rate of church membership growth, it is consistent with the economic and social conditions of the present time. Large families are no longer an economic asset, as they were on the farm. It is estimated that it costs the average middle class family $85,000 as of 1980 to rear a child to the time of graduation from college.[6] In addition to the economic limitations placed on large families, the scarcity of living space in apartments and urbanized environments make it less appropriate to have large families. Consequently, family planning and birth limitation are coming to be accepted values. As long ago as 1950, it was noted that resistance to birth control was weakening in the church. In a questionnaire study (Bittinger, 1951, page 110) of three hundred three Brethren pastors (representing a 73.7% return on a mailing to four hundred seventeen individuals), it was found that two hundred twenty-five pastors (74.3%) did not object to the use of contraceptives on a religious or a moral basis. On the other hand, 14.5 percent did object on such a basis, and 11.2 percent refused to answer the question.

The American family is frequently described today as oriented toward economic consumption rather than to production, as was the farm family of the previous century. No precise comparisons of Brethren family consumption patterns as compared with American families in general are known to the author. Consequently, any estimates given here are intuitively based upon unsystematic observation and therefore are subject to refutation. Do Brethren families differ significantly in their patterns of consumption of goods as compared with the patterns of their immediate communities? Among the older Brethren, the values of frugality, the simple life, nonconformity to the world, avoidance of display, the refusal to promote class distinctions in dress and lifestyle were strictly upheld.

---

[6]Thomas J. Espenshade, "Raising a Child Can Now Cost $85,000," in *Intercom, Population Reference Bureau, Inc.* Vol. 8, No. 9, p. 1.

The issue embodied in this problem may be exposed readily. Are these values positively *taught* today in the family setting and in the church? Are they *observed* in actual life patterns? The answer appears to be that they are not widely emphasized in teaching anymore and are not markedly observed in actual practice. There are, however, some regional and local exceptions to this generalization.

Rather than to suggest the solution or the direction which the church should take in these matters, it would seem appropriate for this chapter to remind the church and its individual members of the need to decide whether the values in question are worth conserving. If so, why? And how can they best be expressed in church teaching and in community and family life? Shall wasteful consumption and unnecessary display continue to be avoided? Is there a genuine value in the principle of the simple life and in moderation and avoidance of excess in materialistic consumption? Do these values fit consistently with an outgoing ministry of service to nations and peoples less fortunate than we—ministries which require money which we are asked to give?

The growth of public and higher education in the past fifty years has resulted in the removal of the young from the home for a large percentage of the daytime hours. This means that they are exposed to the influences of a wide variety of ideas, values, and norms among their peers and their adult contacts. All of this makes more difficult the maintenance of "peculiar" or distinct patterns by the church and the family. If there is a desire to retain distinctive values and life patterns, it should be recognized that this will not happen automatically or without serious effort. The social and the cultural influences in the mass society toward leveling lifestyles are great. There are other influences at work to produce class and clique distinctions in the American community. If these trends contain elements which are to be combatted by the church, positive family and church counterinfluences must be generated. Perhaps the role of the church today centers not so much in keeping separate from "the world" but in entering into the secular order as individuals, family units, and congregations to counter those trends which produce injury, suffering, loneliness, fracture, and alienation.

This discussion might be extended indefinitely to include other important aspects of change in the Brethren family today. The reader may wish to ponder issues related to the rise in divorce rates, the sources of family unity in the mobile and increasingly fragmented family, the rise in delinquency, drug addiction, and illegitimacy, and the revolt of the young. Do these trends indicate some degree of failure within the American family and church to help youth to relate wholesomely to the pressures and crises of modern life? If so, in what ways can the church and the family succeed in the areas where the failure rate is increasing?

Also of interest is the analysis of new values which are being accepted by families today. These are myriad—too numerous even to list fully here. What are the potentials for family unity and personal development which can be derived from increased emphasis upon companionship, sexual fulfillment, personal growth, leisure, and camping and traveling together? How can the mixed effects of television be handled? Are the new goals of child-rearing being utilized: intelligence, social skills, vocational preparation, better education, personal development, emotional maturity, and self-fulfillment? Most of these child-rearing goals would have been questioned formerly. Although we take them for granted, do we effectively pursue them?

Some Dominant Themes in Church Life Today

In the midst of an increasingly prosperous, industrialized, and sophisticated society, the patterns of church life could not escape the efforts of change any more than could those of the family. Our purpose does not permit an extended analysis of these changes. Only a few major trends can be mentioned. The reader will be able to think of many which could be added to the discussion.

A quick glance at modern church buildings serves well to illustrate our point. The simple rectangular buildings of the past seem no longer to serve the complex program needs and the esthetic interests of present-day congregations. Today churches are being designed to combine beauty, a worship-inducing atmosphere, and a variety of functional and practical uses. They are expensive, but it is difficult to make comparisons in terms of value of materials and energy utilized in construction of churches of the past and now on a per-capita basis.

Apart from the cost and the architecture, an underlying change in thinking and values as well as in overt church activities is indicated. We appear to be using our church buildings much more and for a greater variety of activities. Since this is true, the numerous architectural innovations appear as a response to a felt need and serve specific purposes. Simplicity as a value in church architecture, however, can still be expressed in meaningful ways. These ways will certainly take on a mode different from that of the past. It would seem consistent with Brethren values of the past for building committees to examine well their motivations in selection of architectural styles and furnishings. Is avoidance of wasteful expenditure, display, and class distinctiveness still important to us? Church architecture can still express our style of life!

Changes in religious organization and pattern have been frequently analyzed by making use of the "sect-church typology." This has only very limited use in considering a single denomination since it is a generalizing concept designed to organize data of many religious bodies. Some insights from these studies[7] may be illuminating for our purposes.

In the past, our denomination possessed more of the attributes which comprise the idea of a sect. Some of these were: an unspecialized and nonprofessional ministry, a high value placed upon inner religious experience, a strict adherence to biblical standards, a moral community excluding unworthy members and regarding themselves as God's elect, a renunciation of the world with its prevailing culture patterns, and simple worship and organization.

Currently, our denomination exhibits many of the attri-

---

[7]The reader may consult for further study: Liston Pope, *Millhands and Preachers,* Yale University Press, 1942, pages 122-124; and Bryan B. Wilson, "Analysis of Sect Development," *American Sociological Review,* Volume 24 (February 1959), number 4.

butes of the church rather than of the sect. Some of these may be listed: greater prosperity of the membership approximating that of the middle classes, less rejecting of some aspects of the surrounding culture, acceptance of members on the basis of ritual conformity rather than on demonstration of inner religious experience, an educated, professional full-time ministry, and complexity of worship and organization.

Recognizing the need for flexibility through a team approach in the church's response to mission and the desirability of structural overhauling, the Annual Conference of 1968 authorized a thorough reorganization of the commissions of the General Board and the church headquarters staff positions, to be completed by September 1, 1969. The number of commissions was reduced from five to three. As a result of revamping and retirement, between one-third and one-half (*Messenger*, May 22, 1969, page 18) of the staff was replaced. Many positions and job designations were created or revised, while others were dropped. Our leadership today possesses a promising combination of youthfulness, skill and creativity of approach. Combined with greater adaptability in organization, our denominational program offers both an innovative style and a renewed dedication to the fundamental task of the church.

Our discussion of trends in the life patterns of the church today has been greatly abbreviated and selective. It is meant to be suggestive only. Excluded but potentially fruitful for examination are other aspects of our contemporary church life such as the role of Christian education at the congregational, college, and seminary levels; the care of the aged; trends in district and local church organizational patterns; professionalization of the ministry; camping; and relations to other denominations. Perhaps these will suggest further thought and evaluation on the part of the reader.

In Retrospect

Our rapid survey of several aspects of the lifestyle of the Brethren, past and present, has revealed change in the church at every level. Our lives are lived in a world in which change is a constant factor. It is unrealistic to think that the church could be unaffected by its changing surroundings. Indeed, it is doubtful that the church could have either survived or maintained a meaningful ministry without responding to changing conditions from within and without.

On the other side, where is humankind to find stability and permanence if not in religious values and in faith in God? Granted that the church has changed in the past and will change in the future, what is the source of its firmness and permanence? Is there not needed a fine balance between those values which are changeable and those which are not?

There is no predigested answer to this question. It needs to be faced with integrity and courage by every generation. Each age must discern the gospel for its time. Of course, there are stable and permanent values which are applicable in every age. The Spirit of Christ embodied them *for his time and ours.* With Christ, the church today must be sensitive, loving, concerned, and deeply involved in the human condition. It must be closely tuned to those situations in people and societies that really matter. Any changes in church life that can enable the church to bring the healing reconciliation of Christ to people more effectively should not be arbitrarily rejected.

This does not mean that we should depart from the worthy values of our heritage. Perhaps our greatest contributions will come out of those values to which we have held closely in the past. But this does not call for rigidity or fixing in our lifestyle and patterns. Rather, the best of our effort and our ability must be devoted to the task of translating those values into an effective and convincing witness in the modern world.

The Church of the Brethren in Today's World

In the previous chapters we have stressed the fact that pervasive changes have taken place in the life and the culture of America in the past sixty or so years. These transformations have been as great as any that have ever been experienced in history with the possible exception of changes brought about by violent revolutions and wars. We have seen that these extensive movements inevitably have had their impact upon the church.

The church could not have remained unaffected without taking the extreme road of withdrawal and isolation. The Old Order Brethren are an example of this mode of adaptation. The attitude of withdrawal is essentially alien to the original spirit of the Brethren. They rejected it in the monastic movement of Beissel at Ephrata and repeatedly in the social-service programs of the church.

The church has remained in contact with the changing order in which it found itself. The consequences of this have been mixed. Our segment of the Brethren movement has grown into a moderately active and outward-turning organization. On the other hand, some major values and emphases have been weakened or lost in the process of accommodation to the American culture. Some of these weakened values are nonconformity, simplicity in life and worship, humility, church discipline, faithfulness to literal interpretations of the New Testament, the free ministry, and strict standards of church membership. Some may now believe that these are either expendable or subject to redefinition and to more relevant forms of expression today.

In this chapter, we shall take a look at the church in the eighties and as it moves toward the beginning of the twenty-first century, little more than fifteen years away. What are the needs of people in the modern world? And what is the role of first century, little more than fifteen years away. What are the needs of people in the modern world? And what is the role of the church in meeting those needs? Does the church know itself and what its mission is? How shall the church discover itself and its mission?

Denominational Identity Crisis

The processes of change and development within society and therefore within the church have not slowed down or ended. If anything, they are more rapid and confusing. They are always more apparent to the old than to the young who tend to take the present conditions as being the historical ones.

In addition to the direct consequences of this change and adaptation, a more subtle problem has arisen. It is the loss of confidence and certainty about our denomination's identity in today's world and its role in the world of the future. Partly as a result of rapid change and partly as a result of sophisticated modes of thought which have entered into the lifestream of the church, we are no longer entirely sure as to *who* and *what* we are as a denomination.

Our situation is analogous to the problem of the boy who has become painfully aware of changes in his body which mark the transition from childhood to adolescence. These transitions are frequently accompanied by a changing self-concept and by new roles and relationships with which he is unfamiliar. Self-doubt, uncertainty, and anxiety are sometimes associated with this period of rapid growth.

During the 1960s and 1970s, a comparable situation existed within our denomination. Many voices in Christendom

were describing the Christian church at large as hopelessly irrelevant to the modern world and too rigid bureaucratically to
change and respond to those needs.

There were those within the Church of the Brethren moving toward this view. Some were saying we must work outside
the church or with other means to meet the needs of these
radically different times. There was debate and polarization of
opinion concerning the trends which the church was taking.

One segment, more closely in contact with the ideas and
traditions of the more conservative churches in the East,
called the church to be true to its heritage as revealed in the Bible. This group, including the Brethren Revival Fellowship,
sought to preserve the old doctrines and values against compromise and change. They have worked within the church
toward the goals of deepening their own commitment to these
values and toward winning new followers to their viewpoint.

On the other hand, a young and vigorous group sought to
enlarge the church's involvements in ecumenical and interde-
nominational relations. Not primarily concerned with the con-
servation of the traditional image of the Brethren, they sought
to adapt its methods and its ministry to a different order of
concerns. Some persons in this wing were convinced in the
1960s that the Church of the Brethren should merge with other
denominations and seek to make its witness felt jointly with
them. They perceived denominationalism as a weakening and
fragmentation of the Body of Christ and as contrary to his will.
It is clear that their conception of what the church should be
was different in a great many respects from that of the right
wing.

Still another group, perhaps the greatest majority,
remained on the middle ground between these two positions.
Many in this group are deeply committed to working within
the church to develop innovative programs toward a ministry
relevant to our radically changed world. Their leaders, while
not anti-ecumenical, sought to see the church affirm the most
sacred and applicable values of our sectarian background.
They believed that the Church of the Brethren has much to offer other denominations and the world at large out of our
heritage—especially in our peace witness and service motif.

They took the position that our denomination could best fulfill its mission by remaining a separate entity within Protestantism while at the same time working and growing with other denominations toward a more active and varied ministry to the world.

During the 1970s, the church literally rediscovered its heritage. A strong demand developed among the members for books and other materials dealing with the church's past. Brethren authors, stimulated by both the growing interest in our heritage and by a policy of encouragement by The Brethren Press, turned out literally dozens of books and numerous articles in *Messenger* and *Brethren Life and Thought.* Study guides and study materials developed for groups to use in local churches had a wide circulation. Perhaps not unaffected by the fact that the nation as a whole was looking to its own heritage as it prepared to celebrate its two hundredth anniversary in 1976, our denomination seemed to be expressing growing awareness of its own rich background and saying, "We are Brethren."

Undoubtedly much needs to happen if the church is to continue to develop its identity. Many members remain on the periphery of the church's life. Others, while attending worship services more or less regularly, have yet to involve themselves seriously in the discovery of the church's place in their own lives or the modern world. They remain, alas, nominal Christians.

Sources of the Church's Identity

Therefore, the church must continue to work at these questions. What is the church? What is its mission in today's world? How can we strengthen our sense of *being* the church and *knowing* the Christ who is its Lord? Let us examine several basic sources of the church's identity and mission.

First, our present and future contribution to the world will continue to arise necessarily out of our historical background and from what we have become now through the historical process. We could go the direction of severing our connections with our sectarian origins. But if we do, we shall undoubtedly also be cutting ourselves off from some of those elements which represent our contribution to the world.

Our membership can recover a significant source of religious identity by maintaining continuity with our spiritual heritage. We can conserve those portions of our heritage which comprise essential elements of the New Testament message to the world today. Durnbaugh (*Brethren Life and Thought*, Winter 1965, pages 54-62) has suggested that these elements from our heritage are: pacifism, the simple life, and the unity of life and worship. Norman Baugher (quoted by Durnbaugh in the above article) has stressed the following points as values from our heritage: the relation of religion to life, Christian Pietism, the particular pattern of our church polity, ordinances and practices offered as an evidence of our conception of the nature of the church, and serving as a conscience among the churches on matters of peace and brotherhood.

Renewal and recovery of purpose can come to the church as we rediscover these and other crucial aspects of our vital heritage and as we redefine and reinterpret them for today. The church will not likely be able to make a significant impact for Christ by discarding its heritage or by severing its continuity with the past.

This principle does not prevent the church from cooperating closely with other denominations in program building. Even organizational merger does not necessarily imply the loss of values from our heritage. Ideally, merger should take place between denominations whose doctrines and values are compatible with each other. Sharing and implanting these values within the merged denominations could then take place. Our doctrinal heritage could be preserved and, more importantly, serve as a leaven. This could take place only if both the leadership and the membership of the church were consciously and fully awakened to those aspects of our heritage which are to be preserved and if they were faithful enough to testify and witness to them continually.

A second source of the church's identity and renewal is the New Testament and the life of Christ. This is the same source which produced the renewal movement known as the Protestant Reformation and later the Anabaptist and Pietistic movements. It was the source for Mack and the seven who participated with him in the first Brethren baptism. It can be the source of our renewal of covenant with God in Christ today in a very different kind of world. The church cannot play down this primary foundation of its existence. The New Testament is always relevant and vital. Only our interpretations and customary responses to it are sometimes dated and inappropriate.

The essential element of the New Testament is not undeviating belief in the correctness of all the doctrinal interpretations which have arisen around it. Rather, it is faithfulness to the Spirit of Christ as that Spirit expresses God's will and speaks to the universal problem of our human condition. It was this desire to be faithful which motivated the Schwarzenau Brethren. Today, the desire to be faithful to Christ must not be based upon obedience for its own sake. In our age, it must arise out of the conviction that the way of Christ and the Spirit of Christ are adequate and self-fulfilling in the modern setting just as they were adequate and self-fulfilling for Mack and for countless other Christians of every period.

A third source of identity and renewal for the church is the maintenance of a sense of community among the Brethren both at the local and at the national level. In times past, the cohesiveness of the Brethren has been strengthened and maintained on the basis of a consciousness of kind arising from Germanic folk peculiarities and the sharing of powerful religious beliefs. Other sources have been a strong family life, economic interdependence in the rural community setting, non-conformity to the world which succeeded in maintaining a more or less uniform distinctiveness separating the Brethren from other Christians and from worldly people, and at times a unity engendered by persecution by the state. All of these were powerful means of building and sustaining a sense of community.

Today, these sources of group identity are weakened or missing. Annual Conference still serves as a significant expression and vehicle for keeping alive our collective identity, but there are those who in the name of efficiency and economy wish to reduce the frequency with which the Annual Conference meets. In any case, the annual and district conferences are only one source of a sense of denominational integrity. Other sources need to be utilized both nationally and locally.

At the national level, *Messenger* and the scholarly journal, *Brethren Life and Thought*, are vital in maintaining a denominational consciousness for the general membership and the pastor-teacher segments of the membership respectively. Other media of communication are serving their respective readerships.

At the local church level, vital worship and community involvement are needed. As our society becomes more depersonalized in its community setting, congregations are finding increasingly useful the orgainzation of small groups in which serious study and intimate sharing build a basis for enduring fellowship and deepening of the spiritual life. The role of small groups becomes increasingly crucial as congregations become larger and the individual feels less needed or less important to the whole. In the cultivation of cell groups for depth study and personal growth, the church will be recovering a valuable part of its Pietistic heritage which harks back to Schwarzenau where Mack and his associates met over a prolonged period for small group study of the New Testament and church history.

It would appear unlikely that, as congregations grow in size and as competition from other community organizations increases, group identity and loyalty of members can be as intense as in former generations.

The family as a significant source of identity within the religious community ought not to be overlooked. In recent generations, the American family has tended to decrease its religious functions. Strong family life in which religious values are given high priority is a most effective way of maintaining the sense of denominational and congregational loyalty among the young. If the family fails in this respect, the church can scarcely hope to succeed.

The congregation will need to experiment and innovate in its effort to find workable ways to build up and sustain the loyalty and the cohesiveness of its membership.

Occasionally, pastors or other church leaders consciously or subconsciously become involved in building up strong ties of loyalty to themselves rather than to Christ and his church: Such pastors may be frequently quite successful in building up remarkable support and in adding to the membership. Occassionally, some of these strongly motivated leaders are unaware of their ego involvement in their success. Unwilling to recognize when their ministry in a congregation should be concluded, they become involved in cultivating personal loyalty in order to remain employed longer than they ought. In such situations, the congregation faces serious disruption and conflict. The people align themselves for or against the pastor. The larger values of loyalty to Christ and the well-being of the congregation are lost in the bitter anguish of controversy. Mature and wise pastors possess sufficient self-awareness and self-knowledge to avoid cultivating too strongly the emotional ties of the members in a selfish way.

A fourth major source of the church's identity and renewal lies in its ability to relate to the needs of people in today's world. Of the reasons for God's action in Christ's reconciling love and for the church's existence, none would seem more basic than a redemptive ministry to persons. It is in fulfilling this role that the success or the failure of the church in human life stands or falls. And yet, it is at this point that the modern church is receiving some of its most telling criticisms and undergoing some of its most anguished self-examination. Accusations of superficiality and irrelevancy in the church's program—whether justified or unjustified—have seldom been heard as frequently as in recent years.

It would be easy to attempt to counter these criticisms by employing traditional theological concepts and the abstract language of religion. Perhaps this has its place and needs to be done. On the other hand, it is more important to examine seriously the question of the relevancy and the effectiveness of the church's efforts in the carrying out of its central role. This requires a discussion of the nature of human need in the contemporary setting in which we live and work.

Spiritual Needs

In terms of our present program emphases, spiritual needs are acknowledged. In order that our discussion might achieve a necessary balance, they are included. The church's program at the present time is geared primarily to these needs. Emphases change, and no longer does the church stress "saving souls" for the hereafter as its sole task to the neglect of other needs. Indeed, this was essentially alien to the early church.

It is well to point out that the spiritual nurture of the local membership is a prior task of the congregation and the denomination. If there is a failure here, outreach and a vital ministry to people outside the church can scarcely get started. Increasingly, the church regards a spiritual ministry as a ministry to the "total person." This is a healthy trend. It is not valid to entertain a dualism of body and soul—to minister to the spirit and disregard all other human problems. The temptation of the church, however, has always been and still is to be content with the spiritual nurture of the congregation and to separate itself from the more concrete and immediate needs of people both inside and outside the church.

Theological Needs

The church today is in the throes of an intellectual crisis. Never before has there been such a wide range of viewpoints and diverse thought patterns in the membership. Nearly every church located in an urban, semi-urban, or college or university setting is faced with conflicting and unlike modes of thinking. The impact of scientific forms of thought which stress cause-and-effect relationships has caused large numbers of people to think differently about the Bible than do those of more traditional background. Some minds grapple with the implications of evolutionary theory, the class structure, and international politics while others are alienated by discussions pertaining to such matters in a religious setting.

Our pastors are highly trained in theology and biblical analysis in one of the finest seminaries in the nation. Upon taking up small rural parishes, they find that it is necessary to communicate with the "common man" who often has less than a college or a high school education. Laity and clergy frequently are sharply divided in intellectual training and language skills. Such problems are not insurmountable but they do lead occasionally to frustration and dissatisfaction on the part of the parish or of the pastor.

Another level of this problem lies in the world of colleges, universities, and frontiers of knowledge. Advancements in scientific fields pertaining to life, evolution, society, medicine, and the natural world have tended to put religious and theological language into a compartment by itself. Reaching a landmark of sorts in the 1960s, this intellectual crisis has produced the "Death of God" theology and extensive questioning of nearly all religious concepts among both Christians and non-Christians. At the same time, because of this controversial trend of a few theologians and because of other factors, the average aperson has become much more interested in theology and in its importance to the Christian church. It is a hopeful sign when persons seek to grapple intellectually with these and other issues.

Clearly, the intellectual needs of humans today are great. They lie in the area of reconciliation of the rapidly expanding body of knowledge with religious concepts and language. Theologians are actively involved with some of these issues, but inevitably there is a serious time lag. Meanwhile, the person in the pew may get along as best he can by separating even more the religious world from the everyday world of reality.

No easy solution to this problem is offered. New ideas are always controversial; therefore they are frequently avoided rather than confronted. Theological floundering becomes the lesser of evils. More active involvement with theological issues in the colleges and the seminary and in the church publications and curriculum may be helpful. Even this approach may injure and alienate some who are mentally unready to confront the implications of new knowledge or new social issues.

Identity through Involvement in Mission

A fifth source of the church's identity is involvement in mission. As members commit their resources, participate in the successes of the church's effort to minister to people and come to celebrate the joy of service in the name of Christ, questions and doubts about identity can recede into the background.

In the past, significant elements of our denomination's identity came from this source. When asked to describe their denomination, members will often include elements of the church's ministries such as Brethren Service, Brethren Volunteer Service, Heifer Project, and the peace witness.

The challenge of the church today as it builds its mission for the 1980s and toward the beginning of the twenty-first century will be to discover those urgent areas of human and world need to which it can best minister out of its heritage related strengths and areas of expertise.

This is no small task. It calls for clear understanding of the nature of the world as it is today and its needs trending into the future. Great sensitivity to God's leading and to the call from Macedonia on the part of not only our leaders but our members will be required. The place of the Church of the Brethren in the twenty-first century will be dependent upon how the church responds to this call in the 1980s and the 1990s.

This process is already underway in the 1980s. The goals for the 1980s have been projected by the Annual Conference. The church is not on the sidelines. It is engaging already in mission. Now, innovation and creativity mark its entrance into new programs and areas of mission. Several areas of the church's mission today are calling us to deeper commitments and involvement.

A quick glance at the tables of contents of the Annual Conference Minutes and perusal of the General Board Reports for the past ten years give a good idea of the areas of concern of the denomination in the recent past. One is immediately impressed in several ways. The board reports vividly describe the church's program involvement in a complex, world-wide mission which grapples with human needs in great variety. The Annual Conference Minutes reveal the pressing concerns of local churches, the special committees, and the Conference body in the struggle under the leadership of the Spirit to create a fitting response of the church to the modern world and its needs.

The list of concerns is long: Christian lifestyle for the 1980s; keeping the family whole, yet dealing realistically with the fact of brokenness and divorce; the complex issues surrounding abortion; human sexuality; nuclear wastes and nuclear plants; noncooperation with the military draft; use of alcohol and tobacco; equality for women and minority groups; refuge resettlement; the challenge in the mission field; questions of theology and church doctrine; authority of the Bible; ordination of ministers; voluntary service; wealth and possessions; criminal justice and prison reform; law and order; justice and nonviolence; world hunger; life support; labor problems; war and peace, and so on.

A Hindu scholar once gave careful study to the Bible and summarized his reaction by saying that he could find nothing religious in it. In glancing over the above list, members from some traditional religious groups might respond similarly—with some obvious exceptions—that there is little that has to do with religion there. As one member recently responded within hearing of the author concerning a recent sermon he had heard, "We need more religion and less politics in the sermons!" Those who were tradition bound said similar things about our Lord as he sought to make the religious values of his day relevant to the life needs of the people.

A look at the way in which the denomination conceives of world mission today—and the trends of the last decade or so—is instructive of the attempt to relate to a changed and changing world.

The program of missions itself has been continuously evaluated and modified in order to adapt it to changing circumstances. In 1955, a major shift turned the program away from implicit paternalism in our form of administering missions toward indigenization. As a consequence, the next twenty-five years led to the development of independence, a leadership which is nearly totally conducted by nationals, to merging with other religious bodies and a role by the Church of the Brethren of consultation, cooperation, and supplying of resources.

In 1981, after three years of study, a new direction for mission was set by Annual Conference. A broader concept of mission with strong emphasis on mutuality was adopted. This means that, even though our church and its workers are highly educated, rich by comparison with Third World persons, and from a nation thought of as powerful and sometimes even imperialistic, our workers will seek to relate as equals, receiving ministry as well as giving. Decision making and resource allocation will be mutual and democratic. A central objective is to establish churches which are self-propagating, self-governing, and self-supporting. As missions become independent, personnel and resources are freed to be used in new areas and even in the United States which is also perceived as a prime area for evangelism.

Another aspect of world mission is seen in attempts to relate to basic injustice and root causes of social, economic, and health problems experienced in other lands. Perceiving that the treatment of symptoms—the band aid approach—is totally inadequate, mission today seeks to engage in activities which will change outcomes. The denomination carries on health, nutrition, educational, and agricultural programs ranging from behind the Iron Curtain in Poland to China, India and Nigeria, and southern Sudan, and Latin America.

Although innovative, non-traditional and often ecumenical, such programs often receive enthusiastic response from the membership at large—as in the case of Lafiya and the village wells and nutrition program in the southern Sudan.

The church's ministry through the New Windsor Center has been enlarged by the addition of new buildings, facilities, administrators and more broadly conceived ideas of mission. The center administers refugee resettlement, disaster response programs, SERRV which assists people of Third World countries through the selling of handcrafts in the United States, interchurch medical assistance, clothing and blanket relief, and an ecumenical world conference center.

World peace continues to occupy a central place in the concern of the church. Today we are increasingly linking injustice to the problems of recurring violence and poverty in various places throughout the world. In the fall of 1982, a major two-or three-year study of political and economic justice began which will impact in the future on the ways the denomination shall conduct its world peace and mission program. Already planned are specific goals such as witnessing to our own nation concerning justice and public policy, attempts to engage in reconciliation in situations of tension and conflict involving governmental agencies, and calling into question at least five conditions and/or structures which violate the sacredness of persons either on the national or international scene. Such thrusts have been incorporated into the objectives of the General Board.

Of increasing concern to the denomination is evangelism and church growth within the United States. As a result of numerical decline since the early 1960s, Annual Conference commissioned a comprehensive study of the reasons for the decline and the ways to counteract it. The findings of this study which were adopted in 1981 have already become a vital part of the church's mission in the eighties—to realize a growth rate of three percent each year. This challenging goal, however, is not merely a desire for more numbers. It is a desire to bring the renewing presence of Christ more fully into our congregations and to strengthen the witness of Christ by establishing new churches. To this end, the Parish Ministries Commission is committing major resources in the form of loans, grants, and personnel for training of leaders and program development.

A bold, new thrust in program, called the MICAH Mission, was launched in 1982. Taking its cue from the prophet's administration to "do justice, love tenderly, and walk humbly," the church seeks to carry out its MICAH Mission in a wide-ranging effort which includes continued ministries in and to public and private institutions of education, health and welfare; overcoming racial and sexual inequality and injustice; entering into mutual relations with other churches and denominations in Latin America; assisting churches in urban ministries; cultivating spiritual renewal and discipleship through a greatly expanded program of Bible study, prayer and worship in local congregations; strengthening global mission through providing staff and study resources; strengthening family life, adult and youth ministries; and in implementing a comprehensive strategy of Christian education.

An objective assessment may in no way describe our denomination's worldwide program as irrelevant or uninvolved with the major problems of the modern world. The traditional concerns of Brethren—obedience to the principles of the New Testament, desire to witness to Christ's reconciling love, Christian lifestyle, service to others, and peace—are readily evident. Although this summary is far from complete, enough is described to show the general trend of involvement.

The Brethren of the last decades of the twentieth century seek to strengthen their congregations, their leadership and their organizational structure in order to bring the Christ known to Alexander Mack into the modern world. Although our church founders would not recognize the world in which we live today, they could share the enthusiasm we have for the MICAH Mission, the desire to minister both materially and spiritually to the needy, and the concern for lifestyle which motivate the Brethren today.

Conclusion

Our survey of the Church of the Brethren from its founding to the present has been all too brief and certainly inadequate. Enough has been said to show that the church has traveled a great distance in time and space from Schwarzenau in 1708. Its movement has not always been consistent with the purpose of the founders, but more often than not, the church has been true to the spirit of the founding community.

Our calling today, however, is to be faithful not only to Alexander Mack, but—and this is far more important—to Jesus Christ. Our hope is that we can be true to both. But our prior commitment is to Christ. As the church moves through history and translates the mission of Christ into contemporary terms, let both God and all his people be blessed through its ministries!

Materials Cited

Ankrum, Freeman. *Alexander Mack the Tunker.* Scottdale, Pennsylvania: Herald Press, 1943.

Ankrum, Freeman. *Sidelights on Brethren History.* Elgin: Brethren Press, 1962.

Beahm, William M. *Studies in Christian Beliefs.* Elgin: Brethren Press, 1958.

Bender, Harold S. *The Recovery of the Anabaptist Vision.* Scottdale: Herald Press, 1957.

Bergstresser, P., and S. H. Bashor. *The Waynesboro Discussion.* York, Pennsylvania: Teacher's Journal Print., 1880.

Bittinger, Emmert F. "The Church-Family Relationship in the Church of the Brethren Across Two Centuries" (unpublished Master of Arts dissertation, University of Maryland Graduate School), 1951.

Bittinger, Emmert F. "The Simple Life: A Chapter in the Evolution of a Doctrine" (*Brethren Life and Thought,* Volume XXIII, Number 2, Spring 1978, pages 104-114).

Bittinger, Foster M. *A History of the Church of the Brethren in the First District of West Virginia.* Elgin: Brethren Publishing House, 1945.

Bowman, Rufus M. *The Church of the Brethren and War.* Elgin: Brethren Publishing House, 1944.

Brethren's Tracts and Pamphlets, Volume 1. Mount Morris, Illinois: Brethren Publishing Company, 1892.

Brumbaugh, Martin G. *A History of the German Baptist Brethren in Europe and America.* Elgin: Brethren Publishing House, 1899.

Chronicon Ephratense. Translated by J. Max Hark. Lancaster, Pennsylvania: S. H. Zahm and Company, 1889.

Dove, Frederick D. *Cultural Changes in the Church of the*

Brethren. Elgin: Brethren Publishing House, 1932.

Durnbaugh, Donald F. *The Brethren in Colonial America.* Elgin: Brethren Press, 1967.

Durnbaugh, Donald F. *European Origins of the Brethren.* Elgin: Brethren Press, 1958.

Durnbaugh, Donald F. "The Genius of the Brethren" (*Brethren Life and Thought,* Volume IV, Number 1, Winter 1959, pages 4-34, and Volume IV, Number 2, Spring 1959, pages 4-18).

Eshleman, Robert F. "A Study of Changes in the Value Patterns in the Church of the Brethren" (unpublished Ph.D. dissertation, Cornell University Graduate School, Ithaca, New York), 1948.

Espenshade, Thomas J. "Raising a Child Can Now Cost $85,000" (*Intercom,* Population Reference Bureau, Inc., Volume 8, Number 9, pages 1, 10-12).

Falkenstein, George N. *History of the German Baptist Brethren Church.* Lancaster, Pennsylvania: New Era Printing Company, 1901.

Fisher, Virginia. *The Story of the Brethren.* Elgin: Brethren Publishing House, 1957.

Flory, John S. *Builders of the Church.* Elgin: Elgin Press, 1925.

Flory, John S. *Flashlights From History.* Elgin: Brethren Publishing House, 1932.

Funk, Benjamin. *Life and Labors of Elder John Kline the Martyr Missionary.* Elgin: Brethren Publishing House, 1900.

Gillin, John L. *The Dunkers.* New York, 1906.

Henry, J. M. *History of the Church of the Brethren in Maryland.* Elgin: Brethren Publishing House, 1936.

History of the Church of the Brethren of the Eastern District of Pennsylvania. Lancaster: New Era Printing Press, 1915.

Holsinger, Henry R. *History of the Tunkers.* Oakland, California: Pacific Press, 1901.

Kurtz, D. W., *et al. Studies in Doctrine and Devotion.* Elgin: Brethren Publishing House, 1946. Eighth printing.

Kurtz, Henry. *The Brethren's Encyclopedia.* Columbiana, Ohio: Haven, 1867.

Littell, Franklin. *The Anabaptist View of the Church* (second edition). Boston, Massachusetts: Starr King, 1958.

Longenecker, Steve. *The Christopher Sauers*. Elgin: The Brethren Press, 1981.

Mack, Alexander. *Rites and Ordinances and Ground Searching Questions*. Ashland, Ohio: Century Printing Company, 1939.

Mallott, Floyd E. *Studies in Brethren History*. Elgin: Brethren Publishing House, 1954.

Miller, Donald. "The Influence of Gottfried Arnold Upon the Church of the Brethren" (*Brethren Life and Thought*, Volume V, Number 3, Summer 1960, pages 39-50).

Miller, D. L., and G. B. Royer. *Some Who Led*. Elgin: Brethren Publishing House, 1912.

Miller, Howard. *Record of the Faithful*. Lewisburgh, Pennsylvania: J. R. Cornelius, 1882.

Moyer, Elgin S. *Missions in the Church of the Brethren*. Elgin: Brethren Publishing House, 1931.

Qualben, Lars P. *A History of the Christian Church*. New York: Thomas Nelson and Sons, 1942.

Royer, Galen B. *Thirty-Three Years of Missions*. Elgin: Brethren Publishing House, 1913.

Sappington, Roger E. *Brethren Social Policy*. Elgin: The Brethren Press, 1961.

Sappington, Roger E. *Courageous Prophet*. Elgin: Brethren Press, 1964.

Two Centuries of the Church of the Brethren: Bicentennial Addresses. Elgin: Brethren Publishing House, 1909.

Willoughby, William G. *Counting the Cost: The Life of Alexander Mack*. Elgin: The Brethren Press, 1979.

Willoughby, William G. "The Beliefs of the Early Brethren" (unpublished Ph.D. dissertation, Boston University Graduate School), 1951.

Winger, Otho. *History and Doctrines of the Church of the Brethren*. Elgin: Brethren Publishing House, 1919.

Ziegler, Jesse H. *The Broken Cup*. Elgin: Brethren Publishing House, 1942.

Discussion Questions

Chapter 1

1. What were the major dissatisfactions of the reformers and others with the Catholic Church?
2. Why did most reformers from the Waldensians to Luther and Mack stress the authority of the Scriptures?
3. In what ways did the nature of the church-state connections work to prevent reform of the Catholic Church and later the Protestant movement?
4. Why did the Catholic Church oppose reform?
5. What conditions in the Protestant churches called for reform?
6. What needed reforms and changes does the church oppose today?
7. Do you think there is any similarity in our attitude today toward those who call for new programs to grant Blacks and the poor more rights and benefits and the attitude of the established church in the seventeenth century toward reforms called for then? What are they?
8. What do you think might have happened if the Protestant Reformation had not taken place?
9. Could the reforms needed have come about without radical groups and radical protests? How?
10. What were the principal concerns which guided the Protestant Reformation?
11. Do you have a greater sense of kinship toward the Lutherans and the Reformed as a result of seeing the relationship of the Brethren to the Protestant Reformation?
12. Is the authority of the Bible as important today as it was to the Reformers? If not, why not? Are there other important sources of inspiration, knowledge, and authority?

13. What is the implication of our common heritage within the Protestant Reformation for the ecumenical movement today?

14. What do you think would happen if churches or the government today would attempt to suppress or persecute reform movements such as Students for a Democratic Society, NAACP, Student Nonviolent Coordinating Committee, student revolts on campus, "death of God" theologians, etc.?

15. In what ways does this chapter illustrate how God works his will?

Chapter 2

1. How was the early Brethren group in Europe able to grow so rapidly in spite of attempts to suppress or hinder it?

2. Was it either wise or necessary for Alexander Mack and his associates to begin a new church? Might it not have been better to work for renewal within the established churches?

3. Was Mack's separation from the Reformed Church of only his own choosing? Or were official church intolerance and repression part of the reason for it?

4. What were the reasons for the differences of opinion which developed between the Schwarzenau Brethren and Hochmann? Were Hochmann's concerns valid or prophetic in any way?

5. What are the most important values which Pietism upheld? Which Anabaptism upheld?

6. Do you think Mack and the others were able to foresee the dangers and the problems to which the first baptism at Schwarzenau would lead?

7. How can the church regain some of the missionary fervor which Mack manifested in his journeys? If we cannot become enthusiastic about church membership, what should we become enthusiastic about? What aspects of the church's mission deserve enthusiasm, sacrifice, and commitment today?

8. What attitude and behavior brought about the schism at Krefeld? How might this have been avoided? Was Naas's

Krefeld? How might this have been avoided? Was Naas's behavior above reproach? Was Liebe's?

Chapter 3

1. What do you feel was the most important factor in the delay in organizing the Germantown church?
2. Do you think that Beissel's criticism of the Brethren that they were becoming materialistic in Pennsylvania is justified?
3. In what ways did the missionary enthusiasm and activity differ in Pennsylvania from that manifested in Germany?
4. How do you explain the ability of Beissel to attract prominent Germantown Brethren into his movement?
5. Why did the early Brethren hold their worship services exclusively in their homes and barns until 1770?
6. What conditions were regarded as important and generally necessary before Brethren would settle in a new community in the period of their southward and westward expansion? How does this compare with the factors modern Brethren take into account when they move?
7. What were the most important factors leading to the continued rapid growth of the Brethren in America to 1890?
8. What aspects of the growth of the Conestoga church would be applicable to the growth of Brethren congregations today?
9. Do we tend to accept without question the evangelistic method of "revivalism" without seeing it in its historical perspective—as primary a nineteenth-century American Protestant phenomenon, strange to the methods of the early Brethren?
10. In what ways is the debating period of the Brethren (1870-1920) similar to the various forms of dialogue being engaged in by denominations today? In what ways different?
11. Why were the Brethren so long and so slow in becoming engaged in foreign missions?
12. Why has the growth of the Church of the Brethren slowed during the past two or three decades? What can be done to counter this trend? What options does the church have?

Chapter 4

1. Why is it important to examine the ways Brethren are doctrinally in debt to other denominations instead of stressing exclusively our "distinctiveness" and our "uniqueness"?

2. Should we be Protestants first and Brethren second or vice versa? (Of course, we should be Christians first, but let's not avoid the implications of the question!)

3. Do you think Figure 1 is a good model to use to represent the doctrinal relationship of the various Christian groups included?

4. Have the Brethren stressed enough in the past the Protestant character of our beliefs and doctrines? Or have we seen ourselves mainly as "peculiar," "set apart," and "distinctive"?

5. What aspects of Anabaptist and Pietist beliefs do we accept today? Which reject?

6. Would you reject the same aspects of Pietism which Mack did? Why?

7. Do you think the Brethren should revise their doctrines and beliefs and republish them in an unofficial form? If so, why? Or why not?

8. Do you think Brethren today should readily be able to explain doctrinally why our church was founded? Why was it?

9. Does the fact that the Brethren in Europe were "doctrinally fluid" at first and later became rigid and legalistic in America have any implications for the church today? What are they?

10. Although the Brethren in the nineteenth century became rigid and legalistic, did this prevent massive change in practice and belief from coming about? Why not? What does this suggest to and for us?

11. Is there any end to doctrinal change? Do we need some stability and unchangeability in our doctrines?

12. What aspects of the "social gospel" are worth preserving for today?

13. What is the doctrinal role of the Brethren in the ecumenical movement?

14. About which doctrines, beliefs, and practices can young people become enthusiastic?
15. To what shall Brethren be *obedient* today?

Chapter 5

1. To what extent was the lifestyle of the early Brethren due to religious beliefs? To what extent to their German background, their rural way of life, frontier conditions, etc.?
2. To what extent does our lifestyle today reflect our religious beliefs or lack of religious beliefs?
3. Do the questions posed on page 108 have greater significance now that you have read the chapter?
4. Is the lifestyle of the early Brethren more consistent with their religious ideals than ours is today?
5. What elements of our lifestyle are worth going "all out" to conserve from our heritage? Which are not?
6. How can Brethren family life be strengthened?
7. How can Brethren church life and worship be made more meaningful?
8. How can Brethren conserve some form of "mutual aid" in today's more impersonal and more individualistic society?
9. Is the church becoming too bureaucratic and institutionalized? Could our mission as a denomination be accomplished effectively without specialization of tasks and hierarchical ordering of denominational structures?
10. How is the restructuring at the church headquarters enabling the church's mission to be carried out more effectively? What is meant by the team approach at the General Board level?
11. What will the Brethren lifestyle be like in twenty years? Should the church attempt to modify trends in lifestyle? How?

Chapter 6

1. In what ways do you disagree with the discussion of the denominational identity crisis? In what ways do you agree?
2. Do you believe that the church will ever gain agreement

again as to her nature, role, and function? Did she ever have harmony of viewpoint on this issue?

3. Would you add any others to the discussion of sources of the church's identity?

4. What do you think that the effect will be of working closely with other denominations in councils of churches and cooperative projects?

5. In what areas do you suggest that our denomination work with or relate to other denominations?

6. Do you agree with the discussion of human needs described on pages 132-138? Would you list human needs differently? How?

7. Do you agree with the author that in its concern for people the church must move beyond a ministry only to individuals and must work with organizations, institutions, agencies, and power structures?

8. Would you suggest going about this ministry differently? How?

9. The author suggests that the newspaper contains an agenda of work for the congregation. Do you agree? What is the danger in "letting the world write the agenda for the church"?

10. Is it immoral to gain and use force for accomplishing our purposes in today's community? Is it necessary? Is persuasion better?

11. Should the church become involved in community issues even if such involvement *always* produces controversy and hard feelings in the church and the community? Is there a better way?

12. Is it valid to use Matthew 18:15-17 in relation to the community power structure?

13. What else would you include in a discussion of the Brethren mission in today's world?

Index